The Cross

The Cross

Meditations on the Seven
Last Words of Christ

Morton T. Kelsey

PAULIST PRESS
New York/Ramsey

Library of Congress
Catalog Card Number: 80-82086

ISBN: 0-8091-2337-1

Published by Paulist Press
Editorial Office: 1865 Broadway, New York, N.Y. 10023
Business Office: 545 Island Road, Ramsey, N.J. 07446

Printed and bound in the
United States of America

Contents

In memory of my mother
Myra Tripps Kelsey
who knew and lived
the creative way of the cross

Introduction

Human beings have no greater power than imagination. If one enters imagination on the other side of silence, it can take that person to the center of life and reality. How tragic it is that we so often confine our imaginative meditation to human love and beauty and do not extend it to divine love. Gerald Heard, in his introduction to a series of sonnets on James Nayler's last words, speaks of "affirmational meditation" and how much it is needed in our world. He hopes for "a summer lit not by the human but by the Divine Sun." Seldom can an individual come to his or her potential without first imagining that possibility.

In my book *The Other Side of Silence* I have provided a method and rationale for undertaking the inner imaginative journey. In the following pages I share my own imaginative lingering at the cross of Christ. It is much more difficult to write of the emotion aroused by divine events than in the case of human ones. One who writes about reactions to the divine is always in danger of falling into sentimentality or triviality. I believe that it is worth the risk, however.

And why take the cross as a place to begin meditation and story and imagination? Because nothing characterizes the essence of Christianity more fully than the empty cross. Even the resurrection is meaningless without the cross which made it necessary. I know of no other religion that faces the problem of human agony and pain and suffering as does Christianity at its best. We Christians are not advised to get off a hopeless world and forget about its problems, but rather to turn toward the cross, pass through the suffering and come to a victory which transcends suffering.

The cross stands at the center of Christianity as suffering so often stands at the center of many lives. The cross offers a way through our agony, a transformation of it, a victory over it. How can I appropriate this victory? I cannot unless I face the reality of the cross. Thinking is not enough. But in imagination and story one can touch the meaning of Jesus' crucifixion and be resurrected. In these pages I present an imaginative venture into the world of the cross and beyond it to the glory of "the white rose," as Dante described his vision of God at the end of that fearful journey through hell and beyond.

Morton Kelsey
Gualala, California
Advent 1979

Part I
GOLGOTHA:
SEVEN MEN AND
SEVEN WORDS

A.D. 29 Golgotha

A chill wind was howling and tearing the blossoms from the almond trees. Night was falling. A wild night it promised to be after such a violent day. The earth still quavered occasionally from the aftershocks of the great earthquake which had rent the veil of the Temple a few hours before. In the fading light the great masses of dark clouds stood even more menacing against the horizon. Silhouetted against this sky stood three empty crosses, and at their feet were gathered seven figures, four men and three women.

There was no reason to remain. The crucifixions were over. The soldiers had done their gruesome duty and departed. Even the rabble who had come to watch the cruel spectacle were scattered. One body, that from the central cross, had been taken down by a pious Jew, who had placed it in his own tomb nearby. Friends of the other two crucified men had also come and removed their bodies.

It was neither the place nor the kind of day for standing idly by, but they stood there, these seven. Each seemed wrapped in his or her own thoughts, still caught in what they had just witnessed. They were complete strangers. Finally and with difficulty they were moved to speak to one another in hushed tones, and not of other executions they had witnessed. They spoke of elemental things that mattered deeply, of things they seldom spoke—of life and death, of hope and meaning. They were like men and women newly awakened out of a long sleep; their eyes opened for the first time. They had shared a common experience. A new and shattering depth of reality had opened to them. It shone as a strange light in the eyes of each.

These seven formed a motley group. Closest to the cross stood a Roman centurion, Claudius Pretonius, and next to him the last person you would ever have expected to see so openly exposing himself to capture, Jonathan, a well-known Jewish insurrectionist. Facing these two and talking with them was Hannibal, a Phoenician merchant who ordinarily would not consort with such common men. Even more surprising was the presence of the scion of a powerful priestly family standing next to the Phoenician. Baruch was the young priest's name. A little apart from the four men stood three women. Julia, the Syrian courtesan, was well known in the less savory quarters of Jerusalem. In rapt conversation with her were a wealthy Arabian princess come to Jerusalem for her health, Balina by name, and a slovenly looking Hebrew woman from one of the poorest sections of the city.

Whatever could have drawn this unlikely group together on such a day?

It was the cross before which they stood. A young man had been crucified there and something

4

in the manner of his dying had affected each one of them profoundly—the very center of their beings had been touched. He had spoken only seven times in the six hours that he hung there. Each time he spoke, his words had pierced deeply into the heart of one of those who now stood before his cross. These seven had come there for different reasons, several to watch the execution out of idle curiosity, another forced by profession to be there, while one other had just happened by. An unearthly power had caught each of them, snared them, transformed them. They were not standing there, talking together, by chance.

There was nothing especially unusual about crucifixions. The Romans often used them to bully subject peoples. Three was a smaller number than were ordinarily crucified at one time. Once twenty years before near the little town of Nazareth the Romans had nailed up two thousand men, women and children for a petty uprising. Every adult Jew had sometimes seen the crosses bearing their victims standing stark against the sky. What was it about this particular execution which arrested the attention of these seven human beings and changed them, drawing them into a group beneath that cross in the gathering dusk of an ugly day? What was it? It is very difficult to say, but stranger still is the fact that millions have been touched during the two thousand years since, as they have quietly turned inward and stood listening at that Cross. These seven were but among the first.

From the point of view of the casual observer there was nothing particularly unusual about what happened there that day. One man did show remarkable courage, it is true, especially in the light of the events which led up to his crucifixion. These three men were well known to many of those who watched.

Gestas, Dysmas, and Jesus of Nazareth were sentenced for political conspiracy. Two of them had been members of a fanatical group which made raids on Roman supply trains and desert outposts. These men had been caught in the act, brought to Jerusalem and speedily sentenced. The third man, Jesus of Nazareth, was convicted of leading a dangerous political party and of pretending to be the rightful king of the Jews. Obviously Rome would not tolerate that. His sentencing had been more complicated and protracted.

The Temple guard had seized him in his nightly hiding place with his followers. One of the band had betrayed his master to the authorities for thirty pieces of silver and led the captors to him there. A brief fracas ensued. A servant of the High Priest was injured. The disciples fled in terror and the prisoner was seized and hurried off to an illegal night session of the Sanhedrin, the Jewish high court. After a trial which everyone agreed was a farce, he was declared guilty of blasphemy, of pretending to be the Son of God or even God himself. Since this was an offense subject to the death penalty, the High Priest turned him over to the Romans for sentencing and execution. Only the Romans could administer the sentence of death.

Early Friday morning the prisoner was led before Pilate. He presented a poor appearance, for he would not defend himself. He stood silent before the governor, almost as if he were the judge rather than the accused. Pilate did not want to pass sentence. There was a rumor that he tried to turn the man over to Herod Antipas since he was a Galilean, but Herod was a foxy one and after a travesty of a court scene with his drunken courtiers, he sent the man back to Pilate.

Pilate had never been distinguished for his clemency, but yet for some strange reason Pilate wanted to let the man go free. It might have been the pressure of his superstitious wife and a dream she had. In any event, the High Priest finally brought pressure to bear, and since Pilate had already been in trouble with the Emperor on their account, he dared not oppose them. Sometimes the Romans granted pardon to one man at the Passover; so he made one last attempt to save the man by asking the crowd whether they wanted Jesus or Barabbas pardoned. The crowd, egged on by the retinue of the High Priest, asked pardon for Barabbas and in regard to Jesus cried out: "Let him be crucified." Pilate sentenced him to death.

Crucifixions were grim affairs. They can't be recast for kindergarten children. First, the prisoners were stripped and scourged with lashes set with little pieces of bone and metal. The victims could barely stand after such a flogging. It was then that the soldiers had their sport. In this instance, since word had it that one of the criminals claimed to be a king, they took him, placed a red Roman cloak about his shoulders, thrust a reed into his hand and pushed a crown of thorns down upon his head. Then mocking him, they pretended to do obeisance to him. Finally wearying of their sport they redressed him, and he was led with the other two out of the Praetorium up the narrow street to Golgotha, or the place of the skull.

As an added indignity the three men were forced to carry the heavy cross beams of their own crosses up the steep hill to the place of crucifixion.

Weak from the scourging, they often needed help along the way. One of the prisoners fell three times, and finally a bystander, a black man from Cyrene, was pressed into service to help him.

On Calvary or Golgotha (the place of the skull) the three uprights stood awaiting the cross beams and their victims. The prisoners were stripped of clothing, given a draught of numbing gall, which the one named Jesus refused. They were then fastened onto the cross beams by nails driven through their hands. The beams were hoisted and attached to the uprights; the feet of each man were nailed to a projection jutting from it. Finally a titulus was hung above each prisoner's head bearing the crime for which he was being executed.

The condemned were not elevated far off the ground, as later ages have surmised, but rather only a foot or two. The curious crowd pressed very close, milling, pushing, jeering, having sport. The High Priest and his company were there and took occasion to taunt the prisoner whom the Sanhedrin had condemned. The clothes of the dying fell to the soldiers, who divided some of it and cast dice for the better pieces.

Crucifixions were usually noisy and violent. The pain was excruciating. Often the crucified screamed and cursed and cried out. The men on the two outside crosses were no exception. They cursed everyone and everything and even took up the gibes of the High Priest against the prisoner on the central cross. Hours went by. It was this, the almost unending agony which made crucifixion such a dread torture. Sometimes the victims would linger three or four days, dying by inches.

The central figure spoke only seven times

from the cross. Some of his statements were so unusual that some people thought he might be deranged. He said: "Father, forgive them for they know not what they do." In replying to the question of one of the men being crucified with him, he said: "Today thou wilt be with me in Paradise." He looked down upon his mother and a friend and said: "Mother, behold thy son. Son, behold thy mother." He was silent for a long period and then in utter desperation cried out: "My God, why hast thou forsaken me!"

Later he cried out: "I thirst." This was a common complaint for the crucified. The loss of blood caused a traumatic thirst which was almost unbearable. A young priest soaked a sponge in his own sour wine and gave him a drink after this cry. About three that afternoon, the man called Jesus cried out: "It is finished," and "Father, into thy hands I commend my spirit." After that he spoke no more. It was indeed finished.

About noon the heavens clouded over and the sky grew black. There was heavy thunder and much lightning. The crowd hurriedly began to disperse, fearing a violent storm. At about three o'clock there was an earthquake.

The next day was to be the passover Sabbath. The High Priest requested that the business be hurried along so that the bodies might be removed so as not to defile the holy day. Dead bodies were defiling to the Jews. The governor issued the order for *crurifragium*, the breaking of the legs by hammer blows. The prisoners then died quickly for reasons that are not understood by medicine. When they came to Jesus of Nazareth they found him already dead and did not break his legs, but thrust a spear into his side instead. Joseph, a well-known and wealthy man of Arimathaea, a member of the Sanhedrin, obtained permission to take Jesus' body down and bury it in his own tomb in a garden nearby; he completed the task just at nightfall.

These are the cold, bare facts of what happened on the Friday just before the passover Sabbath during the priesthood of Caiaphas. On the face of it, it would seem difficult to understand why so many have turned back again and again to these events and found such power in them. These seven men and women stood talking quietly in the gathering dusk around the central cross after all the others had left. They were gathered at the world's fulcrum in the fullness of time. Each had a story to tell. The seven stories tell what really happened there.

Claudius Pretonius

Claudius, the Roman centurion, was not a bad fellow. He loathed the job which he had to do this day, the scourging of three prisoners and their execution. He was a far more sensitive person than one would expect a man to be with a task like that to do. It took all the guts he had to carry it through. Being a Roman in a land where Romans were hated and feared was not easy for him. He abhorred Palestine and all those in it. He despised the cowardly, scheming Procurator, Pilate, and disliked most of his fellow centurions. He disliked the servile, treacherous Jews and their leaders. Most of all he hated himself for being where he was, a representative of oppression. He resented having charge of executions and particularly this one. Two of the men were the usual political bandits, but the third was no ordinary criminal. That was easy to see. In fact, this man's crucifixion was the most extraordinary event he had ever witnessed. What dignity the man possessed! What quiet composure! How had such a one come to this end? The bearing of the man hanging on the cross made his disgust with himself even more bitter, but this was his job. Pilate had pronounced sentence. There was nothing else to do.

If these poor devils had been Romans, he thought to himself, there would have been none of this torture. It was forbidden to scourge a Roman citizen, even if he were sentenced to die. These three prisoners had been beaten until their backs were raw; then, while his duties took him elsewhere, the other soldiers, goaded on by a bully, had taken the least offensive prisoner and sported with him as a cat with a dying mouse. It sickened him, yet what could he do and keep the respect of his Roman Legion? He was supposed to be hard, tough, unfeeling. No, if they had been Romans, there would have been no death march to Calvary, no humiliating exposure of their persons, just quick beheading which was merciful indeed. Claudius sometimes wished for death for himself so that he could escape the wheel of his own inner misery as well as the senseless cruelty around him. He wouldn't blame the Jewish people for any degree of revengeful savagery if they ever did succeed in revolt. He often wondered how he would feel were he in their place. . . . How often he thought over his own failure, his stupidity which had contrived to bring him here. Standing before the cross the past events of his life marched before his eyes like an army in parade.

There was no need that he be in this intolerable situation on this day in early spring in the year 29 A.D. He had only himself to blame. He might have been in Rome even now if he had not been such a fool. Claudius' father had made a mint of money bringing grain from Egypt to the hungry city of Rome with his vast fleet of ships. He went down with the largest of his ships in one of the many violent storms. He should have known better than to sail at that time of year. He was driven to make a fortune. He succeeded, for he left an estate of a thousand talents, a huge fortune.

Claudius had been only ten then. His father had always been so busy with his shipping that they rarely saw one another. Yet he idolized his father and had treasured the fleeting moments they had together. Still, sometimes as he grew older he resented the fact that his father had not managed to give him more time. It was now sixteen years since his father's ship had gone down and still he longed for him and missed him. His mother had always worshipped his father. When he was gone, she turned the same single-minded devotion upon her only child. She sold the remaining ships and settled back to the villa, where she continued her comfortable, decent, but shallow and godless life.

She had no depth of mind or spirit with which to guide a growing boy. She had long ago rejected the old, inherited, pagan cult as beneath her contempt, and philosophy was over her head. She lived no particular belief, unless you can call "eat, drink and be merry for tomorrow we die" a form of conviction. Her one desire was to keep her son happy and she used all of her resources toward this end. He could have anything he desired. Claudius took well to the central role. Sensing his mother's inner desperation helped him to slip completely into the pattern she made for him. Unfortunately, however, he had none of the moral restraints which she had inherited, restraints which came to his mother from her patrician father's deep but now rejected faith.

During his teens Claudius started to live

among the most dissolute crowd in the sophisticated metropolis of Rome. Gambling, wild revels, courtesans consumed enormous sums. The vast fortune began to dwindle. His mother saw too late what she had done to him and, broken-hearted, she became an easy prey to the Roman summer fever. She died when Claudius was twenty. To escape his own grief and guilt he threw himself into further dissipation. For a few years his star blazed bright in the fashionable circles of the city and then went out.

At twenty-three he found himself penniless, physically and morally debauched, the laughing-stock of sophisticated Rome. For a few months he tried to keep up a pretense, but eventually even the money-lenders learned his true condition. Deserted by his erstwhile friends, alone, he was finally forced to make a living. Thinking that it would be best if he left Rome, he decided to join the army and try to make a fresh start. No one there would know what a fool he had been.

Because he was well-educated, knew his way around, had some good connections, he advanced quickly. In two years he became Centurion Claudius Pretonius. Six months later he was sent to Palestine. While his career there was not flawless, he did achieve a certain prestige. Claudius had never been vicious and the impact of the suffering and injustice into which his new life thrust him brought out the best in him. His restraint was remarkable and, unlike his fellow soldiers, he was seldom consciously cruel and never used extortion on the poorer people. Sometimes when memories pricked their way in, he drank too much, and then he was filled with remorse for what he had done and what he had become. Life was meaningless to him. He was burdened down by guilt which only those who have felt it can understand. He was lost and knew not where his life was leading. "What can anything really matter?" he often asked himself. Claudius was living on the brink of an abyss. He sometimes thought of suicide. For Romans it was an honorable solution when things were intolerable.

When some of the soldiers calling out obscenities started to throw dice for the Jewish teacher's cloak, it angered Claudius more than he could bear. There were *his* soldiers, foul-mouthed, laughing and joking as they gambled for the man's finely-woven robe, while from his cross the victim looked on with compassion. It made him ashamed, ashamed for himself and for his men. Gradually Claudius' attention became riveted upon that central figure. There was none of the fear and hate so apparent in the other figures; there was no suggestion of the violent hatred, not the bitterness and scorn which showed in those other faces. As he remembered now, the man had not even cried out or cursed as the soldiers drove the nails through the fine, strong hands. It seemed miraculous that he had not even uttered a word, not even a groan. What self-control and courage! Claudius had seen dozens of executions and never before had he witnessed anything like this; even the bravest screamed when the hammer fell. Indeed there was a nobility about that face, a powerful repose, even a certain royal carriage in his figure hanging there. His detachment seemed to say to those who tortured him, "You can kill the body but the soul is not within your grasp."

Claudius' reverie was interrupted by a disturbance. His men were fighting. "The dice were loaded!''—several accused the one who had won the cloak. He could not allow a scene here in public. A few quick words and the trouble subsided.

His attention returned to the man on the middle cross, who had now opened his eyes and seemed to be surveying the whole scene with sorrow and yet compassion. His eyes passed from the priests who were railing at him, moved slowly over the curious rabble who mocked and jeered, rested momentarily on the soldiers gambling for his clothes, then passed to the two hanging on either side of him. Finally, he looked at Claudius, or so it seemed to him, and said, "Father, forgive them for they know not what they do."

A criminal upon a cross asking forgiveness for those who crucified him? This was certainly a novel experience. Nothing like this had happened before. If the man had not shown such indomitable courage, Claudius would have thought him demented or a fool. According to the code under which Claudius functioned, hate was a virtue; only idiots and fools forgave. He had been taught never to forgive his enemies but to hate them with all his strength and power. Perhaps this was why he could not forgive himself, because he did not know how to forgive or even how to try to forgive another.

And here was this man offering *him* forgiveness, the legionnaire who had executed the order of death, who had given the signal to drive the nails, who had made the sign to hoist the crossbar to its peg on the upright post. Claudius knew in that moment that what he had just witnessed was no ordinary event. This man had actually forgiven all who had connived and plotted for his death, even Pilate who had weakly consented, and, yes,

16

he had forgiven the curious, morbid crowd who watched for kicks.

"Father, forgive them. . . ." He felt something break within him when he heard these words, something which many persons have experienced throughout the ages, when the words were needed and they were ready and willing to hear. A sense of release crept over him, a feeling that he could not explain nor account for. He sensed in that moment that he had not really been responsible for this execution, any more than he was wholly responsible for the mess he had made of his life. Forgiveness swept through him like a mighty flood, leaving him at peace with himself and with those around him.

He felt a sense of relief in knowing that he need no longer carry this hatred for himself, nor his resentment for his father's busyness and his mother's shallowness. For he had been forgiven, not only for his part in this execution but for all his license and dissipation, and now he could forgive his father for neglecting him and his mother for spoiling him and even himself for what he had done to her and to himself.

He was forgiven . . . the burden of guilt fell from his shoulders. It was a fact. Suddenly he felt himself a different man as he stood watching this figure upon the cross. "Who was he?" Claudius wondered. "He, whose words carried such power, was he indeed only a man?" Claudius felt released, as if a new way had opened and he could start afresh. He was overwhelmed in wonder and amazement the rest of those three hours that he watched. He hardly felt the earthquake. Something was happening within him; a healing was taking place. Forgiveness had unlocked the door and a new path had opened before him. Even his body seemed restored and he breathed more deeply. Is it any wonder that Claudius lingered after the body was taken down? Is it any wonder that when Jesus offered up his spirit with that final cry of triumph, Claudius spoke out, "Surely this was the Son of God."

When they took the body down he sent his soldiers home. He remained. He could not tear himself away. The words, "Father, forgive them for they know not what they do" sang through his head, orchestrated into a mighty symphony. He finally noticed that there were others there also. He was the hated Roman. He wanted to speak to them, but they had to move first. He would not inflict his unwanted presence upon them. He waited.

Jonathan, the Zealot

Jonathan ground his teeth in paroxysms of repressed grief and rage as he watched from afar the threefold execution at the place of the skull. If he had despised the Romans before, it was nothing to the hatred which now devoured him. Jonathan did not know the central figure hanging there, but he certainly knew the other two well, Dysmas on the right and Gestas on the left. Dysmas, his dearest friend, endured the torture better than he dreamed he could have, far better than he himself would ever have borne it. It was only by chance that he, Jonathan, was not suffering on a fourth cross there. For this reason he kept himself safely in the background. Someone might still recognize him. He had no desire to add another tortured broken body to those now there.

The two men whom he knew were no ordinary criminals. They were not brigands who pillaged for their own profit. They were political revolutionaries, patriots, known as zealots. They were a Jewish prototype of Robin Hood and his men. They never touched a Jew unless he were a turncoat tax collector or one who had lowered himself by entering some other service of the Romans. However, they felt no compunction about taking Roman lives, for they were fifth-columnists, underground workers, secretly seeking to undermine the Roman authority. They had done a fairly good job, too. A Roman supply train en route to Jericho now needed an armed escort of cavalry. They were certain they would be enabled to do to the Romans what the Maccabees had done two centuries before to the Greeks who had also tried to oppress the chosen people. They needed only more men to join their underground ranks. Poor, short-sighted young zealots, they failed to recognize the difference between the might of Rome and the weak decadence of that old Greek kingdom.

Jonathan had not known Gestas long, for Gestas was a fairly new member of the group. Some of the men felt uneasy about him, wondering how sincere his motives were. At times they suspected him of using the movement as an outlet for his cruelty. There was always that danger in such groups. The rest of them regretted the methods they were forced to use, but Gestas seemed to thrive on murder and bloodshed.

How different was Dysmas, his dearest friend. They had both been born in the village of Bethany, just a few miles from Jerusalem. They had had a common ancient grandfather who was one of the last survivors of the Jewish state which Pompey had destroyed ninety years before. From their earliest childhood he had taught them about the Torah and the history of their country, regaled them with the fantastic, and yet true, story of how the band of fanatics under Judas Maccabaeus (which means the hammerer) destroyed the much larger armies of Antiochus the 4th. The first thing they learned as boys was a quiet but steady hatred of the Romans who had forced their way in and finally turned their country over to that pig, Herod and his family. Jonathan and Dysmas were both strict Pharisees and both proud of their heritage and their religion, so that the Roman oppression was especially abhorrent to them.

Because of close surveillance, few people had had the courage to join their organization, and so they couldn't risk an open revolt. They had therefore gone underground, sabotaging the Romans in every way they possibly could. The most effective method discovered to date was to attack supply trains. The men waited behind the rocks on the road to Jericho, then swooped down on the helpless merchants hired by the governor, killed them if they resisted, and quickly retreated into the rocky fastnesses where no one could find them. This plagued the Romans and at the same time provided the zealots all the food and weapons they needed. For three years they had operated successfully. Recently, however, there had been a concentrated effort to trap them. Two weeks ago the Romans sent a group of soldiers along the road disguised as slaves; the skirmish did not last long. Seven of their men were killed. Dysmas and Gestas were seized, while Jonathan and two others escaped. It was impossible for the Romans to pursue them far in that wild country.

And so there they were at the place of the skull. Jonathan heard the screams and cursing of his two friends as the execution progressed. He did not blame them for the cursing that poured from their mouths. He was full of it too, but he dared not let loose what he felt. At least they could speak their hearts, something he was craving to do. He watched their suffering and realized the ugly end of their high hopes for their cause. They might as well cry out against their oppressors. There was nothing more that the Romans could do to these friends now, nothing more. Jonathan wondered who the fellow was on the central cross . . . A titulus over his head carried his charge, but it was obviously a buffoonery: Jesus of Nazareth, King of the Jews. Probably a member of another band of patriots like his. There were dozens of them. Yes, but this man seemed different; he wondered about him . . . Why was he so silent? How could he stand the pain? Both of his friends finally turned on this one, hanging between them so silently, and cursed him as well. Jonathan could understand that, for if you cursed everyone and everything, your attention was diverted from your own suffering, making it lighter. But Dysmas soon stopped his railing, even though Gestas continued screaming wildly at the man in the center, "If you are the Messiah, then why in hell don't you get the three of us out of here? You fool, you rascal, try a hand at something practical, you King of the Jews!" And he laughed convulsively between his screams. Jonathan was ashamed; he hoped that the bystanders didn't think they were all like that. Gestas had always had a foul tongue and a streak of swagger in him. He wished he could say something to offset this cruel out-pouring, but he could not without revealing his identity. Just at that moment, Dysmas cried out to Gestas saying exactly what was in Jonathan's heart . . . "Don't you fear God? We suffer here together. We receive the just reward for our deeds, but not this one—he has done nothing wrong.

Leave him alone. Is there no decency in you?'' The railing stopped. Jonathan's heart swelled with pride and love ... This young man, Dysmas, had moral as well as physical courage. His religion was genuine and deep. What a beautiful person he was.

What happened after that was no surprise to Jonathan, for he too had been more and more attracted to the central figure on the cross. He noticed Dysmas' head turning toward the man whom someone in the crowd had called Jesus. Regardless of the danger, Jonathan moved forward so that he could be nearer and hear what was going on and give the support of his presence to Dysmas. His fear was disappearing as he witnessed his friend's courage. Finally he found himself at the very foot of the cross ...

Dysmas was watching Jesus closely now, and gradually a strange light began to shine in his face as he looked at the man on the cross. Finally he spoke to that central figure, ''Jesus, remember me when you come into your kingly power.'' What those words said and meant. Under the stress of pain and suffering we often see things more clearly than at any other time. Some of our greatest revelations are born of suffering. Dysmas had seen the truth. It had dawned on him like a great light. This man *was* the Messiah. His was a different kingdom than they had sought. He and his friends had labored for the wrong kind of goal and they had gone the wrong way. It was through suffering and courage and persistent love that the real kingdom would come. *His* kingdom was the only one that mattered. Hate and vengeance would only delay its coming. It was not too late to change. An about-face, a reversal of life was contained in those words of his. Men and women can so change, and they have been so changed . . . those such as Urban Grandier, who centuries later made the same kind of change as he faced the stake.

Dysmas then saw Jonathan and nodded recognition. And Jonathan watching saw and knew what had happened and, deep in his heart through his love for Dysmas, he too was stirred. It is strange how the faith of those we love can awaken the same thing in us.

Then came the words from Jesus, words that he would never forget, words which ratified what he saw in Dysmas and felt in himself. They were words that could have been spoken only by a Messiah or a deluded lunatic, and this man was no madman. The young man replied to Dysmas, "Truly, I say to you, today you will be with me in Paradise." These words were spoken with such conviction and authority that they rang true. This man knew that Paradise. A great burden was lifted from Jonathan and an awakening faith kindled within him. His friend was safe beyond the threats and torture of any human. He knew it.

It was a strange alchemy which transformed his doubt to conviction. Jonathan's mind and heart probed deeper and deeper into the meaning of what he had seen and shared. New thoughts and images tumbled through his mind. He saw that there was an eternity in which to work things out. Not that he would cease attempting to change his world, but he would discover a better way than violence. He sensed that this new way would often seem futile, but he knew that it was the only way for him . . . the only way to victory. There was indeed a Paradise. Peace and hope crept into Jonathan's heart, peace and victory even in that place of death. His attitude toward the Romans seemed to change as well. This Jesus on the Cross had shown him that hatred was a hindrance. Jonathan slowly looked around him at the Roman soldiers, at the centurion Claudius, and pity swept through him, a genuine compassion. As this man Jesus had said, they did not know what they were doing. They were caught in a mighty maelstrom of forces beyond their control. They had blindly allowed themselves to be swept along, just as he had, only on the other side. None of them had been conscious enough as individuals to question the power-driven status-quo of their time. They were to be pitied, not hated, these Romans. They were caught as he had been.

Jonathan and Dysmas were among the first to discover the miraculous power of the Cross in transforming hatred through the understanding strength of love. These two young men, one in death throes and one with his life before him, were awakened to a new dimension of life. They began to know that there was hope and that paradise could be reached. The world was in God's hands. Hate defeated those who sought the kingdom. Love facilitated it. Bitterness and hatred were washed from them both. They knew that hate robbed them of freedom.

Some sixteen centuries later, the early Quaker leader James Nayler spoke words that touched the same truth. Released from prison he was on his way home when he was robbed, beaten and left half-dead in a field. He was discovered and brought into a house where he died two hours later. Before he died he said these words: "There is a spirit which I feel that delights to do no evil, nor to revenge any wrong, but delights to endure all things, in hope to enjoy its own in the end. Its

25

hope is to outlive all wrath and contention, and to weary out all exaltation and cruelty, or whatever is of a nature contrary to itself." James Nayler had discovered the same Spirit which Dysmas and Jonathan discovered at the cross.

Jonathan lingered on even after the bodies had been taken down. For the first time in his life he spoke to a Roman soldier without contempt or fear. The man standing next to him was Claudius, the centurion. He even found that this Roman soldier was as moved as he. Jonathan was no longer afraid. The Roman told his story. Jonathan told his and they embraced before the cross. They shared "the peace" . . . the peace of God. Then Jonathan saw the others. He brought the Roman with him as he moved toward them. This man had also been transformed, and he told them not to fear him. These two became companions on a new and strange venture. Claudius, the Roman executioner, became the companion of the Jewish revolutionary, Jonathan. Nothing is impossible at the still point where worlds meet.

Julia, a Woman of Questionable Reputation

It may be hard for you to believe, but most of the people who gathered for the executions that first Good Friday had no real business there at all. They were present for only one reason. They wanted to watch a crucifixion. It was an opportunity to live out their blackest and most repressed feelings. They participated vicariously in the horror of it and thus escaped their own inner turmoil. In the historical study, *The Devils of Loudun*, in which he describes a public execution, Aldous Huxley writes, "Before we start to congratulate ourselves on our finer feelings, let us remember, first, that we have never been permitted to see an execution and, second, that when executions were public, a hanging seemed as attractive as a Punch and Judy show, while a burning was the equivalent of a Bayreuth Festival or an Oberammergau Passion Play.... When public executions were abolished, it was not because the majority desired their abolition; it was because a small minority of exceptionally sensitive reformers possessed sufficient influence to have them banned. In one of its aspects, civilization may be defined as a systematic withholding from individuals of certain occasions for barbarous behavior. In recent years we have discovered that when, after a period of withholding, those occasions are once more offered, men and women, seemingly no worse than we are, have shown themselves ready and even eager to take them."

We should not, therefore, condemn Julia too severely for getting up bright and early in order to have a ringside seat at Golgotha. Crucifixions did not take place every day and she had desperate need to escape from herself, for she had become a common street-walker of Jerusalem, a member of the world's oldest profession. A great number of the first Christians were recruited from this profession. Early Christianity had the vitality and the power to effect profound changes in the psyches of men and women. It was rooted in the very nature of God's way with humankind.

Julia, the daughter of Joseph, had grown up in Sidon on the Syrian coast. Her parents had been simple people. They wanted many children but were able to have only one child. Because of this they focused their entire attention upon her, giving her far more than they could afford, far more than other children in her station would normally receive. Her father was a wool-carder, plying his trade at home where the family worked together. They were too close to one another, concentrating wholly on one another with no outside interest whatever.

As for religion, the pagan temples of their city were known throughout the world for their license and corruption. So degraded were they that decency forbids discussion of them any further.

Thus it is not surprising that this little family rejected the traditional religion and, thus, the spiritual side of life. Instead, they lived entirely in the material here and now, enjoying their simple family pleasures, their work together, their afternoons at the quay watching the strange ships arriving from foreign lands. It never occurred to them to look for spiritual sustenance. It was to be found in the Jewish synagogue in Sidon but life seemed pleasant enough without it and these Jews were such fanatics. There was nothing outstandingly bad about these people but they had no depth and, like others with shallow roots, when the storm struck they were like houses with foundations built upon the sand. The sand washed away and the houses collapsed.

Life moved smoothly for this happy, secure little family until suddenly without warning, when Julia was fourteen, her small world went to pieces. One day there were rumors that the plague had struck several people living in dwellings near the waterfront. They saw some strange rats in the alleyway. A few days later Julia's mother was stricken, and then her father also. In four days both parents were dead and Julia found herself alone with no one to cling to and no inner resources with which to go out and fend for herself. She was numb, then thrown into despair, but slowly a rising rage possessed her.

Julia wondered why should this happen to her? She, who had never wanted for anything, who had always been protected and made to feel very special, why should she be so treated? Before long she was even faced with the specter of hunger. Why? Why? Bewildered, helpless, lost, finally in desperation she looked for help.

Her first attempt to find someone on whom to lean proved disastrous. She did not know human beings could be so cruel. The man who pretended to help her merely used her and then dropped her. She was naive and her need was great. Added to desperation and loneliness came the shock of disillusion and disgrace. But again and yet again she was driven to seek someone to cling to. She could not stand alone. Finally she sank so low that she could no longer hold up her head in Sidon. She then fled to the anonymous haven of Jerusalem to hide. There loneliness and hopelessness in time totally engulfed her. No longer naive now but caught in a vicious circle of weakness, bitterness and hatred, she gradually assumed a hard and bitter mask to cover her emptiness and pain. Her name became proverbial among the profession of Jerusalem—"As hard as Julia" they said. How little people knew! In her lucid moments she hated life and hated herself with a demonic fury, but then sank back again into futility.

Is it any wonder, therefore, that she went out early to witness this execution? This was the place of hatred. She could vent her feelings here, escape from her guilt through the spectacle of torture. Julia made a habit of attending all crucifixions. The many fanatic and rebellious Jews in Jerusalem gave her frequent opportunity for this diversion. Lately, the entertainment had begun to pall on her. It had become depressing as well as releasing, but in desperation she had continued coming, and so here she was again.

She watched uneasily but intently. She listened to the screams as the nails were driven through two of the victims' hands. Then the torrent of cursing and obscenity broke from the men.

30

Again vicariously she was able to forget herself and suffer with them, be tortured with them, but her vicarious participation did not last long this time. That man on the central cross bothered her. He was not behaving in the way most of them did. He was silent. Silent! Julia wondered how he could remain silent. What was wrong? He was conscious. He had not tasted the numbing cup and yet he made no outcry. His behavior made her uncomfortable. When the two other victims began to curse God and all humanity, this man in the center blessed them with forgiveness. Unbelievable, incredible, unreal!

Slowly a veil was taken from her eyes and she began to see the scene as it was, as it really was in all its ghastliness. This one man made her see the torture for what it was. She couldn't keep her eyes off him. Now she only glanced at the other two rarely, for this man moved and troubled her, his dignity, his courage. Then her attention was caught by a little group that moved slowly from over by the city wall up to the foot of the crosses there beside her, five weeping women and one man, tall, straight, young. They moved forward silently as though no one else were there. Even the soldiers backed away instinctively as they came forward.

There was a heavy silence, a gathering hush as the one on the central cross looked down upon them and spoke. The slight turning of his head, the movement of his eyes, made clear the one to whom he spoke. First it was to the woman in the blue veil: "Mother, behold your son." And then looking at the young man who stood at her side, he said: "Son behold your mother."

She watched the young man put his arm

around the older woman and give a slight nod of response. There was nothing they could say. Their grief was beyond words.

Julia was carried back in memory to the little room in Sidon where her father lay dying. How similar and yet how different was that scene. Her father had in anguish begged her to carry on, but there was a hopelessness and fear in his voice—no courage nor faith, no hope nor conviction. Yet this man in the midst of his physical anguish and great humiliation was quietly telling his loved ones to go on living their lives, and he did it with power and conviction. It was as if he said: "All is not lost because of this. Life still has meaning and value, yes, even if evil seems to triumph. Because one tragedy has fallen, do not create more by despairing." She could tell by the victorious tone of his voice that what he said was a command, a command which would be observed. She could see the courage and comfort, the strengthening, the revitalization, which came to them from his words. They said nothing, but she knew that they would be going on from this moment strengthened to face life, empty though it might appear to be.

Julia knew how hard it was to go on when one is left behind. Yet, right then she knew that simply going courageously on, one step at a time, would save them as it would have saved her. She realized that humans are most often saved by inconspicuous actions and unheroic deeds. Her task was to turn from her bitterness and walk out into the unknown, confident that within the darkness there will come light for each new step ahead. It was as if this man had said: "Go on, go on in faith my friend and mother, my brothers and sisters."

These words also spoke to her and said: "Awake, my child. There *is* reason even for you to live."

Then a veil was removed and Julia saw a new way revealed. She saw how narrow her life had been, how empty of meaning, how cowardly. Oh, how unlike these two, this woman and this tall young man, she had been. She had thought only of herself and her misery, of how hard the world had dealt with her. How she had pitied herself! She had mocked the parents she pretended to have loved. She had blasphemed herself. She was at least partly to blame. There had been no meaning in her life because no one had ever put it there, and she had never looked for it on her own. Julia had never thought it through before. There was meaning, of that she was now sure. Something in the way this man dealt with those who loved him had touched her. She saw an opening between the worlds.

As these thoughts flooded through her mind she vaguely sensed a shaking of the old foundations of her life and new ones being laid. She felt a strengthening of will, a sense of direction and purpose. Nothing like this had ever happened to her before. She had made resolutions by the dozens, but this time she knew that she was leaving her old way of life and would find a new one. She would seek fellowship and find someone to serve. Her life would yet become rooted and established.

The past few years suddenly began to fade and new hopes opened for her. Life would go on and gather new significance. She knew not exactly how, but, as she lingered there after they had taken the bodies down, she found herself moving over toward the woman in the blue veil saying, "I am not worthy but may I join you and serve you?" Somehow she knew she would not be rejected and she wasn't.

After they took away the body she noticed others there too who had a light of new life about them. They were drawn to one another. Not one of them looked with scorn upon her. They all knew and talked with her as an equal. After everyone had left, still they lingered there. Together they were sharing a rebirth; a new faith was emerging and each in turn was discovering his or her destiny.

The way was not always easy for Julia. Dark days came upon her when she was drawn back toward her former life, but she went on doggedly and did not give way. Gradually she came to firmer ground. It took years before what was begun at Golgotha was completed, but Julia never turned back. Eventually she was victorious.

Julia found, in the implication of these brief words, the courage to go on through the deep waters of personal bereavement and collective tragedy. At the foot of the cross where Jesus of Nazareth spoke consolation and courage to those who faced loneliness and desolation, Julia had a new start. She found people who would not just use her, because they too had passed through agony and found reality. Often she went back in her imagination and heard the words, "Woman, behold thy son. Son, behold thy mother." A spring of hope and new life was running here. Julia drank of it and was reborn.

Hannibal, the Phoenician Merchant

Darkness covered the earth like a pall, and that matched Hannibal's mood perfectly. He couldn't offer any explanation for the strange phenomenon. Had it not been the time of the full moon, it might have been an eclipse, but that was impossible at Passover time. Sometimes storms swept up from the Red Sea so violently that one scarcely saw them coming, but he was sure that this could not explain the sudden menacing darkness, even though he knew how unpredictable the weather could be in that part of the world. Indeed right now Hannibal felt that neither weather nor anything else was dependable. He would in fact have gone even further and said that life was never secure and safe. Hannibal had his reasons.

He had long since come to treasure only one thing in life—money. Six months before he had been a rich and important man. Now he was penniless. It had taken twenty years of undivided attention and toil to accumulate a fortune. First he had traveled the caravan routes himself as a driver through Persia, India, to China. Then he mortgaged his soul for a few mangy camels of his own, then one caravan, then two, and later many more. Finally he had warehouses in all the major cities on the route.

No one imported more of the treasures and delicacies from the East than he. The Roman Emperor's household would have been far less dazzling without the goods which Hannibal imported. Indeed Tibetius had given him special recognition for his service and had bestowed upon him the much coveted Roman citizenship. He wasn't any happier with ten caravans and thousands of talents of gold than he was before, but he was so busy he had had no time to think about that.

And then through a series of misfortunes all of this wealth slipped away from him almost overnight. Had he believed in the gods he would have sworn they were leagued against him.

Several years before he had taken a young man into his employ. Soon the young man won his confidence and later became almost a son to him. Hannibal had disciplined, educated and trained him in commerce and finally had taken him into partnership. For years they had worked together. Then suddenly the young man died. Added to his grief for his only real friend, he discovered that the cash was short. Another took over the accounts. An appalling deceit was revealed. Over the years his protégé had managed to embezzle and squander three-quarters of his fortune.

On top of this, political revolt in Persia had cost him five warehouses and six caravans. Finally when all of his debts were paid, Hannibal was nearly penniless. Times were hard and he was disillusioned, tired and no longer young. He felt he could never rebuild what he had lost. Furthermore now that his fortune was smashed, his wife whom he had treated more as an ornament than a person, left him. Having pursued money as the greatest goal, he had used and often abused his friends, and so no one rose up to aid him. Instead, his former friends avoided him or openly ridiculed him. These Jews had a saying about casting your bread upon the water.

In a last desperate attempt to make a comeback he had gone to Pilate that very morning. The Emperor had conferred the great honor of Roman citizenship upon him just two years before, through his Procurator in Caesarea. There was no problem for a man of his power to get an audience, though Pilate would recognize his plight and his need for some special consideration. His ability was known far and wide. Pilate received him politely, but seemed nervous and preoccupied and except for vague expressions of regret and a little banal conversation he offered nothing.

With no recourse to recoup the one thing that had given meaning and zest to life, he gradually fell into a state of utter despair. Nothing to live for, no one to care for . . . he was at the end of his road and he knew it. On this particular day as he started to walk out of the city gates and down the road toward Jericho, he found himself headed for the precipices which fall in thousand-foot drops to the Dead Sea fifteen miles away, precipices often used by desperate men for self-destruction.

And so Hannibal passed through the gates which led past Calvary. He was so numb with despair that he hardly sensed the excited crowd milling around until he found that he could no longer force his way through the throng of people. Then he noticed the dark sky and the figures on the three crosses silhouetted against it.

Something about the center figure caught his attention. Yes, the man was the Nazarene who had caused such an uproar in the Temple five days before. The poor fool should have known better than to buck the moneyed interests in Jerusalem. Even Hannibal at the summit of his power would not have attempted that. He had listened to this teacher recently himself when he was at a loss with nothing else to do. His heart had almost been touched but he had caught himself in time and moved out of hearing. "A young misguided idealist," he reminded himself. Strange, however, the lift the man's words had given him, the only lift in months.

But for what charge had the soldiers nailed him on a cross? In three languages the charge was written on the titulus, in Aramaic, Greek and Latin: "Jesus of Nazareth, King of the Jews." Hannibal knew them all. He had to in his business. What fantastic buffoonery was this to accuse this man of political pretensions to the throne? No wonder Pilate's conscience had been bothering him this morning. This was his doing, for no one could be executed without his sentence. Accuse this man of that?. . . . Nonsense. True he was a vigorous, headstrong young prophet—a man who spoke courageously of love and freedom, of evil and good, of forgiveness and courage, but that was no political crime. Why, this was an outrage, a miscarriage of justice, but what one would expect in such a world as this. No wonder the sky was black.

Hannibal stopped and sat down upon a stone nearby and ruminated on the irony of it all. He deserved his present lot, for he had ridden over his competitors, misused his wife and friends, but this man. . . . what harm had he done? How tragic this was—an innocent, a godly man being crucified. Just then Jesus spoke out in agony: "Eli, Eli, lama sabachthani! . . . My God, my God, why hast thou forsaken me?" Hannibal listened and thought: Truly, if ever a person had the right to speak these words, it was this man. His only offense was being true to himself in the face of the shallow, grasping temple officials. He had presented an example of a perfect Jew, kind, courageous, faithful, profoundly religious. And they tortured and murdered him between two bandits.

As he sat there Hannibal's own troubles began to shrink in size. He had been thinking that he was in a bad way, that his lot was a tragic one. Why, he had more in just the fine clothes he still wore than this man had ever possessed. He still had health and an able mind and yet here he was setting out to kill himself. In his heart he had been crying out to life, "Why hast thou forsaken me?" "How weak I've been," he thought. "Here is real tragedy, a young man despised and unjustly crucified, whose agony plumbs the very depth of human pain and despair. My trouble is nothing compared to what this man endures."

Suddenly his life fell into perspective. How narrow it had been. He realized that in making a god of money, wealth, and his own achievement he had lost his soul. He had sacrificed everything for this one object and he had missed the whole point of living. He could have saved the young business partner but he had dominated him, lived through him, used him and so destroyed him. He could still have a wife and friends if he had not abused them. The fault was in himself. He had forsaken himself. He began to see his life as this man Jesus would have seen it. Slowly an urge to start again rose within him; a desire to find out what it was this young prophet had been willing to die for became more and more important. Hannibal had gained a whole world and lost his soul. Perhaps one of this young martyr's disciples, perhaps the one who stood there with the woman before the cross, would help him to start to find a new direction. He would wait and speak to him. So it was that Hannibal lingered on with several others after the crowd had slipped away.

Hannibal had discovered a totally new perspective as he meditated there at the foot of the cross and heard that cry of dereliction. Soon he began a new business and was as successful as ever. His home and warehouses were refuges for followers of the way. It was he who first had a silversmith fashion a cross with a body on it and when it seemed that life asked too much of him he would pick up this symbol of real tragedy and his own would shrink in size. Jesus had consciously accepted his destiny. His commitment to God's will had led on to this cross. With these reflections his own suffering was less.

Hannibal's inner agony and emptiness did not simply go away. It was a long way back. The inner darkness still came to him but he would pick up a cross and listen to the words "My God, my God, why hast thou forsaken me?" He was not alone in his deepest agony. He did not stand alone. He knew that one had gone before him, who still was with him, who whispered in his heart "I will give you strength to bear whatever weight of pain or sorrow is laid upon you. I will help you learn from them and overcome them. I will never forsake you."

At Golgotha Hannibal heard a voice coming as from another world: "Take courage. I doubted also when I passed this way before you, and there is light within the darkness." Hannibal learned the real power of the crucified one when he heard that voice in the midst of his personal despair. He glimpsed the struggling God in the midst of his smaller need.

This cry of agony and despair is good news to those who wait at empty crosses. God knows their agony and travail. He once knew them on the cross. They were no small thing. They caused him to cry out. What a comfort to know they have a God who understands their agony and has conquered it. It forges bonds between us which even death cannot break.

Baruch, the Priest

The ugliest episode on that black Friday before the Passover Sabbath was perpetrated by the group of whom you would have least expected it. It is difficult enough from where we stand to believe that the priesthood of the great Temple in Jerusalem were so unaware and corrupt as to bring Jesus to a cross on Golgotha. But it is even more incredible that they would come to taunt him at his crucifixion. These priests, the top representatives of the highest form of monotheistic religion in the ancient world, did, however, seek out Judas and bribe him to show the Temple Guard Jesus' nightly rendezvous in Gethsemane. In addition, they put pressure on Pilate, and used their influence on the mob to which Pilate had referred the sentence. And then they even turned out to watch the man die, and to mock him as he did.

It is so easy to criticize these men. These priests had been intimidated by the Roman government for nearly a hundred years. Under this tension and intimidation they had been forced to compromise so long that the younger priests had come to take compromise as natural and normal.

These priests were the civil as well as religious leaders of their people and they had a grave responsibility. There were many young religious fanatics who rose in desperation with crazy plans to free the chosen people from Rome's domination. These men had to be put down. If the authorities in the Temple failed, then what little semblance of autonomy and self-government which remained would be destroyed by Rome, and the nation would disappear. They were guardians of a very precious heritage. Then too, these priests were very powerful, and power corrupts—and corrupts no one quite as much as religious leaders. Their own wealth and position were at stake. Perhaps this is the clue to their bitterness and taunting. They were afraid and insecure. We must remember also that although they were the top representatives of Judaism, they were not necessarily the best. The Pharisees were really the religious leaders of the people, and the monastic Essenes of the Dead Sea taught a religion which in many ways paralleled that of Jesus of Nazareth.

These men self-righteously convinced themselves, as we do so often, that the end justified the means and that since this young prophet was disturbing the valuable status quo, he must be liquidated as a dangerous radical. Thus they felt that they were serving the cause of religion and of God. Retribution has always been a dangerous instrument in the hands of fallible humans.

Baruch was one of the younger priests who set out together from the Temple. The group arrived at the place of execution just as the three doomed men appeared bearing their crosses. One of the three, they believed, had sought to overthrow the old religious order they represented. They came to stand as witnesses against Jesus as he died. Baruch was no weakling. He had seen men and women die, many of them. It was a hard age, an age of slavery and of empire. This young priest had seen a lot of cruelty, even witnessed other crucifixions. He did not like them. He understood them for what they were meant to be—Roman lessons for the Jews.

Baruch had had every advantage. The priesthood had become a worldly lot and interested in Roman ways. Thus he had been educated as a citizen of the cultured, ancient world as well as in the Jewish law and traditions. Some of the older priests complained about the breadth of point-of-view this wider education gave the younger men. They were beginning to think for themselves and were less loyal to the ancient way. Baruch had shown little evidence of this as yet, for his family was one of the twenty most powerful and privileged priestly families. These families ruled the city, religiously and politically. They were held in awe by the people, who even bowed before them when they passed by on the street.

They were wealthy, too. The first fruits of the land came to them. Their robes of office were more magnificent than even the Roman Emperor's. Sheep and doves and cattle without blemish were bought by the priesthood and sold for sacrifices in the Temple. This transaction provided handsome profit. The changing of money from the Roman and Greek coins which bore an image and were therefore prohibited in the Temple to the half-shekel coins permitted there, brought additional wealth.

Baruch enjoyed the comfort and prestige of his family's office. He accepted it as a matter of course, just as he accepted their conventions and prejudices. He too had been infuriated at the reports he had heard of this young visionary of thirty-three, how he had presumed to cleanse the Temple and speak against their priestly privilege. Although at times in his inner heart he secretly wondered if there might not be something to this man's criticisms, still this man was going about it in the wrong way and was trying to turn everything upside-down overnight. Baruch agreed with his elders that this would only cause chaos and confusion. It was enough to endure oppression without risking a division in their own ranks.

This man was a menace. It was better that one man die, instead of a nation being destroyed. They also convinced themselves that he was fraudulent, as well as misguided. The priests, therefore, had sought, and succeeded in getting the blasphemer condemned, and here they were.

As Jesus was lifted to the cross one of Baruch's fellow priests cried out, "Aha!—You, who would destroy the Temple and build it in three days, save yourself and come down from the cross." A shallow, defensive laughter rang out over the bare rocks of Golgotha. Another priest, the one right next to Baruch, a fellow he did not much like took up the cry: "He saved others. He cannot save himself. Let the Christ, the King of Israel, come down from the cross that we may see and believe." Baruch could understand that this man must be destroyed and that this was the only legal way, but need they make such sport of him? The reactions of his fellow-priests revolted him, and he began to look with sympathy upon the crucified man for the first time.

Baruch could understand that the man had to

die, but why this mocking? If the man were genuine, this mocking rejection would be the worst pain of all. Baruch marvelled at the cruelty of human to human. Baruch had once been left to die in the desert. He knew human cruelty.

Baruch did not take up the cry of the others. Instead he listened and watched and he began to *see*. His prejudices dropped away and he actually *saw* the man who hung there as he really was. Baruch had never seen the young man before. His appearance was far different than he had been led to expect. With his prejudice peeled off he saw a man of real dignity and genuine courage, a man who under the most extreme physical agony neither cried out nor cursed. His words were few. He spoke them well. His incredible attitude of self-containment and peace gradually made more and more of an impression on Baruch. In spite of himself he was drawn to the man. Then he heard the words of physical anguish, "I thirst."

Why through all that torment was it thirst alone that called forth a cry of pain when he suffered so much else? What about the torn hands, the anguished body, the aching limbs? Baruch knew the reason; it struck home to him.

Four years before in the country beyond the Jordan his party had been set upon by thieves. All had been killed except him, and he had been beaten, cut and wounded and left to die in the sand under the burning sun. Hours had passed. One consuming passion grew in him, burned him. He had never known such agony. Just for one cup of water, even for a few drops. What he had experienced was traumatic thirst. Loss of blood created such a thirst. Every other pain had been nothing in comparison. The agony was unquenchable. It remained until the reprieve of unconsciousness.

He understood the unbearable suffering this man endured. Baruch ran and picked up a javelin, put a sponge upon its point and poured some cool, sour wine upon it. He had brought the wine along to slake his own thirst but now he lifted it up to the lips which had just cried "I thirst."

The man drank and looked down at him. What gratitude his look expressed. The community of suffering had made them one. Baruch's spontaneous act of compassion and the relatedness with the dying one that came from it set him apart from the others. His fellow priests seemed to shrink away from him when he returned from this small act of mercy and put the javelin down. This he did not notice but rather kept his eyes riveted on the face that now seemed to him illumined. What they were doing suddenly struck him. This man was no blasphemer, not a radical like the others who had caused such difficulties for the authorities. He was stricken with remorse. Too late, too late to do anything . . . he bowed his head in unbelieving sorrow and penitence.

Now he understood why the others mocked; they were so unsure that they must thus convince themselves. His sudden response to this man and the depth of his own human pain had opened to him a new level of life and had cracked the shell of the old one. Something new was born in him. Is it any wonder that he lingered there after they had lowered the body from the cross? He had served the man he had come to jeer because this man's suffering had struck a chord in his own deepest being. In the most vivid memory of his life, his helpless thirst lying there in the desert, this man was one with him.

It was Unamuno who said that the basis of all real love is compassion, and compassion is suffering mutually shared. It is nearly impossible for a man or woman to love who has never suffered. Baruch had been privileged, protected, living a cocoon-like life, unborn to being a person distinct from the class of which he was a part. However, he had suffered and nearly died. He had tried to forget that excruciating experience on the desert. Yet it was through the crack of his own agony that this man's torment reached him and he was changed.

Baruch knew the fellowship of Christ's physical suffering on the cross, and so was given courage to face his own pain, and then the will and wisdom to comfort others in their agony. He began to see this Jesus as the Son of God, and so he no longer saw a God who looks down in benign detachment, lacking understanding. Rather, he worshipped one who knew the agony of crucifixion and traumatic thirst. Baruch's God knew human agony and cried "I thirst." Baruch was never again at night in pain alone. As he ministered to the dying, his Christ was there, and the words "I once thirsted" came to him through the dark hours bringing compassion, strength, companionship. He told the dying about the voice he heard within his soul, the voice of the Christ. "I thirsted, suffered, but that was not all, not the end or answer, nor for you."

How often Baruch thought back upon those words from the cross. He could never again consciously cause suffering. In this memory of his heart, he saw those lips moving on the cross, those lips drinking up the sponge's brief respite, and then he moved to reach out to human need. He was moved to compassion, to comfort wherever pain had struck, or wherever people's conscious or unconscious inhumanity had caused disaster. The motivation for whole professions stems from Baruch's action: Doctors, nurses, social workers, counselors, many others.

Baruch waited there after they took the bodies down and carried them away. He was so engrossed in his own thoughts that it was long before he saw the other six standing there. He had seen Jonathan once before. The others were not the kind he usually associated with. He went up and spoke to each of them. He knew them because their suffering made them kin. He led them to his house that evening and gave them food, and they talked long into the night.

He told the others his story. He told them how the cry "I thirst" had touched him. He arranged lodging for those who needed it. He watched over that little group until the first day of the week came and confirmed their hope. His kindness, his acts of mercy, did not cease with them. As the years passed by, countless men and women blessed him for his continued mercies. He watched with the dying. He sat beside the sick and ministered to them. He bound up the wounds of those left along the road to die. He carried many cups of cold water. None who appealed to him in need or suffering was turned aside. The words "I thirst" called within his soul and he would get up to look for human need again. When he found some broken human and assuaged that person's thirst he knew that he ministered to his Lord again. Baruch became a legend in Jerusalem, a true priest, a mediator of a much greater spirit than his own. It all started that Friday at Golgotha.

Jezebel, a Jerusalem Housewife

Jezebel never finished anything. Her hovel, in a dead-end alley near the great wall, was always in shambles. Her own person was seldom better. Her hair was matted and her clothes hung in rags. Her children were street urchins, grimy and in tatters. Why her husband put up with her was a mystery to everyone. Her neighbors discussed her situation freely, with liberal additions from their own imaginations, as is so often the case in such neighborly discussions. There was no doubt about it: Jezebel was a mess. The most amazing thing was that Jezebel would most likely have agreed with that statement had she been consulted, and would have laughed heartily because she did not care.

For her life had long ago lost its meaning and had fallen into chaos. She no longer had any honor, nor any friends. She stole what she wanted from neighbors not important enough to do anything about it. She neglected and abused her husband and her children. Being afraid of giving love, she received almost none. She was lonely and miserable, but she affected a nonchalance and a devil-may-care attitude to deceive herself as well as those around her. Everyone walked quietly by on the other side, as we so often do when we encounter people such as Jezebel. It is the easiest solution.

It was true that she had not had much of a chance. Indeed, it was a miracle she had survived at all. After a few years of normal childhood her mother died. For a year or two she was left with anyone who would keep her, and then her father, a crude camel driver, married a woman little better than himself. She resented Jezebel and subjected her to the kind of abuse which struck deep into the child's heart and cut her off from her own feelings and blocked her whole development. Instead of being an object of love she was used by her parents as an object upon which they could hang their own pain and guilt. Thus Jezebel gradually became convinced that she was of no value, and so she abandoned the painful process of growing up. She remained a bitter, spiteful, unhappy child even as her years increased. If some instinct of self-preservation had not induced her to run away and get married she no doubt would have been added to the vast number for whom mental illness formed the only escape from intolerable suffering, the vast horde of demon-possessed found throughout the ancient world.

Off and on a few people tried to help Jezebel, but they soon gave up in despair. This is the tragedy of such people. Very little helps them. They appear perfectly normal intellectually, but they just don't care. Something is lacking in them, so that they don't respond normally. They take what those who offer help have to give and go their way undisturbed and unmoved. From among such people as Jezebel have come the floating criminals of every age.

Everyone had given up on Jezebel as she walked out of Jerusalem that Friday morning to see the crucifixion. She never missed one if possible. They offered real diversion, and this meant more to her than anything else. She arrived early, and found a good seat on a broken column not fifty feet from where the crosses would stand. She had brought along a lunch, for a crucifixion was usually an all-day affair. She did not worry about her children. They could fend for themselves in the streets of Jerusalem. Jews were generally kind to little children. They would not suffer too much.

She watched the laborers prepare the site for the execution. She saw the prisoners stagger up the hill with their burdens. She followed the details of actual crucifixion with tense concentration. The victims on the two outer crosses displayed the usual hatred and agony and provided the morbid thrill she found so necessary. However, the man on the central cross and the words he spoke were distracting to her. She determined to pay no attention to him, but this she could not do. No one could ignore the loud cry of utter desperation he finally gave: "Eli, Eli, lama sabachthani!" When a Roman soldier who thought himself quite well-informed cried out derisively, "He is calling for Elijah, let's see if he will come and help him," she was touched. He was not calling Elijah, but God. She knew that the words he used echoed a psalm he had learned in his childhood. Her own mother had taught her those words before she died.

These words awakened in her feelings long dormant, feelings which reached back beyond the distortion of her later childhood to the happier days of infancy. Her feelings, her attention, were drawn to him. She forgot the others and their screams of pain and anger. Then came his cry of thirst, and as she watched the young nobleman come forward, she too was drawn physically toward that central victim, nearer and nearer until finally she stood beneath his cross. Then he seemed to look directly at her and said these strange words: "It is finished!"

Jezebel was a Jewess. She spoke the Aramaic that Jesus spoke and understood exactly what he meant by these words. Therefore she did not interpret them as a cry of relieved despair as is so often done. These words meant rather that all had been brought to completion, to fruition, to perfection. This man was saying that he had completed the task before him. He had done all that anyone could do. It was finished.

Slowly Jezebel repeated these words, "It is finished." "How could he say that," she thought to herself, "when his career had barely begun?" What mysterious words! They were so strange that her whole being was challenged by them. She began to think for the first time in years, something indeed she had rarely ever done. Perhaps it struck her so forcefully just because she had never finished anything, had always run away from completing any task. Yet here was a young man being tortured and put to death for standing for his convictions, a man whose life was over before it was begun. What had he finished? His was a strange completion.

Jezebel found herself moved as she had never been in her life. A realization began to grow in her that this was no ordinary event, no ordinary man. She tried desperately to recall what she had heard of him. He was a prophet of Galilee. One of her neighbors had claimed that he had healed her child. Her husband had been in the Temple when he called the priesthood a den of thieves and had seen him drive out the money-changers and the merchants from the Temple courtyard. She remembered a discussion at the inn among publicans and questionable ladies, who seldom spoke of such things, about his enigmatic words: "He who seeks to gain his life shall lose it and he who loses his life shall save it." From the forgotten depths of her childhood memories, there arose the image of the suffering servant of Israel. Now she began to see what he meant. Could this be the Messiah? She felt as if she were on holy ground. The foundations of her life shook and trembled.

The Roman soldiers wondered why a frowsy Jewish woman who had obviously come for entertainment now cast herself to the ground, hid her face in her arms and wept so bitterly. Those on the outside never can understand what happens when suddenly a voice speaks within and says: "All of this was for you and such as you. It was for you that he completed his task. He is dying that you might be shaken and live. God so loves you that he allowed even this kind of victory to be suffered through, for you." There is no rational reason why these words of a dying man upon a cross should have this effect, but they did. Many others have found the same reality as they have meditated at the foot of the cross. St. Francis was one, John Wesley another, Augustine of Hippo still another. Suddenly the pressure of God's love becomes so strong that one can hardly bear it, and one changes. One's gratitude is so overwhelming that one thinks with the poet:

> Were the whole realm of nature mine
> That were an offering far too small;
> Love so amazing, so divine,
> Demands my soul, my life, my all.

I wish that I could take you beyond the limits of that day and show you what a transformation those words "It is finished" made in her. Jezebel did nothing which could be termed spectacular, but from the start she made a clean break with the past and attempted to reshape her daily life. It took many months, even years, many ups and downs, before the healing process brought forth fruits, but gradually a genuine love, a kindliness, a naturalness began to grow in her. Her appearance changed. Her children no longer looked forsaken: now and then, her husband was even seen to smile.

Jezebel was amazed that those who waited at the foot of the central cross received her into their company. She was even more amazed later when the fellowship of his followers welcomed her. The new Jezebel recruited far more converts to the Way than a half a dozen martyrs. Anything that could change her . . . When she was asked what had happened, she answered that suddenly she knew, standing at the foot of the cross listening to those words, that this sacrifice had been made for her. The way she told it, listeners did not smile.

I doubt if anything else would have changed her or the thousands like her in her age or ours. God would not have gone to so much trouble in suffering and humiliation if lesser measures would have done as well. For dread disease severe treatment is often required. God in Jesus did all that was necessary and finished the task. Jezebel felt that love, was transformed, and offered thanks to God.

We humans are not as wise as God. We still try to remake Jezebels by preaching at them or teaching them, or if they run afoul of the law, by punishing them and imprisoning them. These methods seldom work. Jezebel could have told us. The story is told of Ignatius Loyola that he once followed one of his disciples down toward the town nearby, when the man was bent on leaving the order and returning to his former dissolute ways. After exhausting every means of persuasion as they walked down the mountain path Ignatius entered an icy mountain brook which crossed their path and said to the disciple: "You go on. I will wait for you here in the water until you return." The friend went on. But the thought of Ignatius risking his life in the icy water haunted him. Finally he ran back and lifted Ignatius out of the water and begged his forgiveness. He was never tempted to leave again. This is what Jesus on the cross did for Jezebel, and what Jezebel did for others.

It is love like that of Ignatius, and even more like that of Jesus—love which is willing to carry through to the finish—that awakens the slumbering souls of Jezebels. As far as I know, it is the only thing that awakens lost human beings. Jezebel knew that this man had finished his way for her, and so she began to grow and finish her task as he had finished his. With this new life and spirit she reached out to others like her in Jerusalem. She found that her example and her love worked the same thing in others that he had worked in her. How often she thought of those words on the cross and marvelled.

Balina, the Arabian Woman

Balina had no intention of going anywhere except home. She neither knew nor cared that on that day three young men had filed out from the Praetorium through the old North Gate on the road to Jericho, headed for Golgotha and crucifixion. Earlier that day she had gathered her camel caravan together, assembled her entourage, and given orders that were to take them back to Arabia. That night they would be in Jericho, even though it had turned so strangely dark at noon that day, and on the morrow they would head toward her oasis home in Arabia. The driver remonstrated with her, but to no avail. To start so late on such a day! Balina, however, was very rich, and this was her private caravan. They would do as she said.

The trip to Jerusalem had been a failure in every way, more heartbreaking and dreadful than she had even feared it might be. She had come for medical help and had received only bad news—the worst news. Naturally she had come to Jerusalem. It was the greatest city near her Arabian oasis, the trade center of that part of the world. It was the city to which her father had sent her to learn of the world and its ways, as even a desert princess must learn. She felt comfortable and at home there.

When her sickness had lingered on for months, and the desert remedies had accomplished nothing, she had decided to seek help, and so she had gathered her retinue together and come to Jerusalem. It was a long and painful journey, but nothing like the misery that awaited her there. Her physician was the finest that could be found, a man who had been trained in the Greek schools. He treated her with violent, ancient remedies. She had been sick and weak before. Now she could barely get about. Finally she demanded the truth and her physician told her quite frankly that although she was just thirty-three, the medical profession could do nothing more for her. She might as well return to Arabia where she would be among her own, and die there as comfortably as possible. To fortify her, he gave her ample supplies of hashish, and directions for its use.

Balina could scarcely face her trip home to her husband and her children. How she dreaded that encounter, to tell them the medical opinion. There would be tears and words of comfort, and oh, the tender care that would be lavished upon her! She wondered if she could bear it for them, and for herself. There she was with everything to live for, thirty-three, and told that six months was all she had to live, and those most likely in agony. She would not let the servants who drove the camels know how dismally she turned her face toward home. It would not become one of her station. She was absolutely alone, with no one to turn toward ... alone, brokenhearted, desperate, sick, facing a journey of three hundred miles on camelback. It was surprising that she even saw the remnants of the crowd still loitering on the hillside of Golgotha. It was a wonder that anything reached through to her dazed mind at all, that any impression made its way through to her consciousness.

Balina had no faith to cling to. She was another of those unfortunate mortals who know much, and yet not quite enough. She believed that the tribal gods, the swift and vengeful spirits of her desert country, were so much superstition. She had learned *that* in the ten years she had lived in Jerusalem, but she had found nothing to take their place. She could not accept the elaborate legalism of the synagogues nor the studied ceremonial of the Temple. She was too highly placed in the social world to become aware of the strong, indigenous religious stirrings which were shaking the common people. To her, life consisted of the things you have, the people who surround you, the here and now. And all this was to be snatched from her. She believed in no afterlife, in no deeper level of reality that reached through to the heart of things.

But Balina was neither effete nor decadent. Indeed, she carried on the finest traditions in which she had been reared—kindness, hospitality, courage. She was a good humanist but like so many modern humanists, who are the nicest people and do the kindest things, she had nothing with which to meet the most overpowering reality in life, the darkness. When death struck at her, she was shattered. Everything seemed to move along well for her until the specter of death appeared and cast its shadow over her and turned life to a heap of dry and broken shards. Gentle rearing was not enough, then. Only a real, vital, personally-experienced faith sustains one in such times, and this Balina did not have. So out of the city Balina went that black, black day. The prospect was six more months to live, suffering and then the end. She was facing death without hope, following a life void of any significant meaning.

The camel caravan passed out of the gates and down the road within a stone's throw of the three crosses on Golgotha. The shock of what she had just learned still stunned her. She had forced the truth from the great physician only that morning and here by 2 o'clock in the afternoon she and the caravan were out of Jerusalem. She heard, "Is it nothing to you, all you who pass by?" sobbed out by several women who stood watching the crosses from the road. These words met her mood and startled her to a greater degree of awareness. She looked from the women to the men on the crosses, two of them writhing in agony, but the third, enduring silently torture beyond description.

Then she heard a cry from that silent one which expressed her whole heart—"My God, my God, why hast thou forsaken me?" The man on the central cross was just about her own age. There was something most unusual about him. She smiled sadly as she read the title: Jesus of Nazareth, King of the Jews. How they mocked him! In Arabia they didn't torture people like this. A glint of recognition passed across her mind. She remembered that she had heard him speak one morning in the city. He was the prophet of Nazareth. He had moved her then. What had he done to be hung up as a criminal? What utter tragedy he was passing through! He faced not only death, but ridicule, abuse, contempt. They mocked his life as well as destroying it. She signaled to the head camel-driver to call a halt and dismounted with some difficulty. She spoke to the weeping women by the roadside. For the first time that day her attention was taken from herself.

"And what did he do to deserve this?" she asked the women. "Nothing," they replied. "He tried to live his life as honestly and courageously as he could." Balina was so intent upon these women, one Jesus' mother, others friends from Galilee, that she scarcely heard the other things he said. Just a few minutes before the ninth hour, she walked slowly over to where six others stood at the foot of the central cross. It was about three o'clock and his face was so tired, she wondered how long he could last. Just then he opened his eyes and gave a great cry, a cry of relief and victory combined. And then, raising his eyes to heaven he said, "Father, into thy hands I commend my spirit." Then he died. It was all over. Jesus of Nazareth was dead.

Balina came late, but soon enough to catch those healing words. "Into God's hands," she wondered . . . "Are there indeed hands into which one may commend one's spirit? Is there one who cares? One who cares for me as my father cared? One who cares for me as the clan cares for one another?" The young man had believed this. Who was she to doubt it? He was not preaching or trying to convince anyone. Those words simply spoke his heart. This was between him and God. This was reality for him. He was so near death that he was no longer attentive to anything but his own soul. He had passed through deep, dark, uncharted waters of feelings, lost and forsaken when the presence of the Father had seemingly been withdrawn. However, that was over now, and he addressed his words simply, straightforwardly to One with whom he had evidently spoken habitually before. Even if unseen, the hands there now received him. She could feel them.

Those were strange thoughts for one who believed nothing. She realized in that moment, as she had never realized before, that her life was only two-dimensioned. She needed an added dimension that this man had, one that reached beyond this life. But could she ever find the faith to say such words as her life ebbed, even on a silken bed? As she meditated there, a steadiness and courage moved within her. His conviction carried conviction into her empty soul, filled it, enriched it. Somehow his belief became hers.

Balina never knew exactly what it was in that scene which brought her to believe, which convinced her, but great deaths have made their mark on other persons as little else in life. One thinks of Stephen, the Christians in the arena, the nameless slaves, the apostles. Almost numberless are those converted by their courageous dying. It is true that they outdied the ancient world as well as outliving it. The blood of the martyrs was the seed of the church. One does not, of course, understand just how, but in that moment Balina's whole life was linked to a deeper dimension, and she became one of the seven who remained at the cross even after Joseph of Arimathaea had taken away the body.

The blackness lifted for her. Indeed a certain lightness and hope took its place. Many people have wondered how the Christians who awaited Nero's soldiers were so lighthearted, carefree.

Well, it was thus with Balina, for suddenly reality opened up to her. She knew that his Father was her Father and he was real. Death could only touch the body. There were realms beyond, and there this Father was found. All was not lost because this world was lost. It is but a preparation for an ongoing. The only argument for an afterlife that really counted was that there was a Father there with hands to receive her, and in that moment she knew something of that Father, and all was well.

Balina lingered on and then later, after talking quietly with the few who stayed, she arranged to meet the other six at Baruch's home. She ordered her bewildered camel-drivers back to the city. Because one life had a fitting end, all life seemed to have meaning for her. Because her life had meaning, she then had a task. She had not long, she feared, to undertake it; so she must waste no time. She started by arranging shelter for the stricken women that night. Then she met the others whose wounds had been healed at Golgotha and listened to their stories. After the events of that first glorious Easter day, she turned her attention to other unfortunates in the city. Six months later, she returned to Arabia. She confounded the doctors, lived another thirty years, rich years, blessed by those who knew her, and blessing all in turn, old and young, rich and poor. Many who received her compassion and ministrations were opened to the Father to whom she witnessed.

"Father, into thy hands I commend my spirit." How often Balina lingered over those words. She watched with many who knew this Father, and she never saw much fear in them as they waited for death. Rather, their lips became still, speaking words like "Father, into thy hands," for they knew that the Father who received them would watch over those they left behind. Her task was to live so that others might see that Father working in her.

She was active up to her death, and met the end with grace and courage and unshakable faith. What courage and hope her words brought to those around her as the light faded from her face and she firmly whispered, "Father, into thy hands I commend my spirit!"

Part II
THE ANATOMY OF GOLGOTHA

Reflections on the Meaning of the Cross

Our journey, empowered by imagination, has taken us back to a bleak, dark day in the year 29 A.D. when three men were led to a hilltop outside Jerusalem and crucified there. We have listened to the stories of seven people whose lives were touched and changed by what happened that day. As I have suggested, this event has continued to change people's hearts and lives ever since, right to the present time.

Why did this event touch the hearts of those seven who walked by the original cross and capture them and change them? Why does that story still have the same power? What is it that draws us back again and again to read that story, to let our spirits hover at that spot?

There is nothing particularly unusual about executions today. They are still a dime a dozen in most places in the world. We have watched in helpless horror as half the population of Cambodia were liquidated and the rest were faced with starvation. We have seen hundreds of the former leaders of Iran lined up and shot. One shudders to remember the millions of Jews who were killed in Germany hardly forty years ago, the fate of the dissidents in Russia, and even more recently in China . . . in Bangladesh and Biafra, in Uganda, Viet Nam . . . The list goes on and on, and there are also the less official executions of war, which are just as final . . .

There have been many, many crucifixions; the Romans, Greeks and Persians used them. Thousands were sometimes strung up in a single day. Ordinarily there would be twenty-five or thirty victims writhing on their crosses all at once.

Why center on this one crucifixion? Granted that this form of death was one of the worst forms of punishment that human beings have yet devised—still, why so much attention to this one crucifixion? Why center on these three men hanging there on the rock of Golgotha at the Place of the Skull in 29 A.D.? What is so different and important about this one particular event that it is worth using our imagination to rediscover what happened there? Why should we spend several hours poring over every detail of this ghastly happening? What is significant about it?

The answer is something like this: The central one of these three crosses is significant because it shows humankind at its worst, and because it portrays the humanity of Christ as nothing else could. It shows what an individual who follows God can do in the face of the black, demonic elements in human nature. Golgotha also shows us what *God does* when such an individual faces

70

these elements. That central cross, when we will face it, first strips us of our complacency, and then leads us toward making a choice between futility and a life of hope and ultimate victory.

The Cross as Naked Evil

The three crosses on Golgotha are one of the best examples of man's inhumanity to man which history offers. Here was a public execution at its worst. Some case may be made for the speedy and private and painless dispatch of certain enemies of society, but here was human cruelty at its deepest and most brutal. Crucifixion was conceived for the sole purpose of making the victim suffer as much and as publicly as possible.

First of all the prisoners were scourged with lashes laden with metal and bits of bone. Then they must carry their own crosses up to the place of execution through the jeering mob which lined the way. Then they were callously stripped of their clothes and held down like inanimate things while nails were hammered through their hands. Then they were hoisted up on the pole so that their feet were just a few inches off the ground, tantalizingly close, and there the feet were either nailed or tied, and they were left to die . . . it sometimes took days. The gnats got into their wounds, into their lacerated backs and into the open sores in their feet and hands. The jeering, laughing, demonic mob gathered to watch the victims writhe and die while gossiping about other crucifixions that they had witnessed and waiting for the victims to cry out. Accusers and enemies often came and stood by and mocked; they could stand right by a crucified one and there was nothing that could be done about it. Sometimes other prisoners picked one victim or another to torment in an attempt to forget their own agony ... A bullfight is merciful to the bull compared to what crucifixion meant to a human being. ...

All this Jesus suffered on the cross. If only one could be alone on a solitary mountaintop one could almost bear it. ... The crowd eating their lunches, the soldiers playing dice, the high priests mocking, the confusion and the noise, the turmoil and the pain. ... One's loved ones there standing by helpless, their hearts breaking, and nothing they could do ... nothing. One could almost have stood the pain alone.

How can humans treat other humans in this way? How can they be so callous, so brutal, so unfeeling, so sadistic and vicious, so cruel and hard ... how, how, how? "Certainly such things could never happen now" we say. I wish that this were the truth but, as Aldous Huxley reminds us, public executions, hangings, burnings, were considered a rare treat as late as they were allowed and brought spectators from miles away. He also reminds us that it was only a small minority who quietly put through the legislation in most countries to abolish them in the last years of the nineteenth century. After the coup in Dacca a crowd gathered in a park to watch the defeated die as the victors lunged at them with bayonets. In China, until recently, public executions were still popular. In fact, wherever the bans have been let down and circumstances have permitted it, we have found people like you and me coming to see others in the agony of suffering and death. . . . How can we account for this?

Fritz Kunkel has said that each of us has underneath our ordinary personality, which we show to the public, a cellar in which we hide the refuse and rubbish which we would rather not see ourselves or let others see. And below that is a deeper hold in which there are dragons and demons, a truly hellish place, full of violence and hatred and viciousness. Sometimes these lower levels break out, and it is to this lowest level of humans that public executions appeal. In the cross this level of our being has thrust itself up out of its deepest underground cellar so that we humans may see what is in all of us and take heed. The cross is crucial because it shows what possibilities for evil lie hidden in human beings. It is the concretion of human evil in one time and place. Whenever we look upon the cross, which was simply a more fiendish kind of gibbet, we see what *humankind* can do, has done, and still does to some human beings. It can make us face the worst in ourselves and in others, that part of us which can sanction a cross or go to watch a crucifixion. . . . The cross is the symbol, alive and vivid, of the evil that is in us, of evil itself.

Scratch the surface of a person and below you find a beast or worse than a beast. (For animals seldom play with their victims.) This is what the cross says. We don't like to believe this, but let's look at the facts. Who were the ones who ran the concentration camps of Nazi Germany, kept the gas ovens fed, made lamp shades out of tatooed human skin, who performed the mass murders and executions? It is important to remember that Germany was the most literate and educated nation in the world. We think that the people who did these things must have been perverted monsters . . . actually most of them, until they stepped into these roles, had been peaceful German burghers who had never hurt a person, living quietly and peacefully in their comfortable homes, and then the devils in them were let loose.

Were all the mongol hordes which followed Genghis Khan just wild brutes? No, at home they were kind and loving to their wives and families, and yet as they swept through Persia they killed a hundred thousand in a single city. . . . Once Attila died, the Huns became as gentle and peaceful as any people in Europe. And yet Genghis Khan, Tamerlane, Attila were novices compared with our educated moderns, much less efficient and adroit at disposing of human life. But when we are reminded of these recent horrors we are prone to say, "Don't remind us. Let's forget." We are loath to read stories of these events, such as Elie Wiesel's little book called *Night*.

We don't want to face our own darkness; it is too painful. The atrocity stories which follow in the wake of every war, every one, involve both sides and are as incredible as the cross, and are usually performed by men and women who never before had done such things . . . scratch the surface of human beings and the demons of hate and revenge, avarice and bestiality and sheer destructiveness break forth. The cross stands before us to remind us of this depth of ourselves so that we can never forget. These forces continue to break forth in many parts of the world now, and many of us would like to forget how in some places in the United States we treat a person whose skin is black. We like to forget Mai Lai and the napalm bombs and the tiger cages in Vietnam.

Again and again we read the stories of violence in our daily papers, of the mass murders that are still occurring in various parts of our land. But how often do we say to ourselves: "What siezes people like that, even young people, to make them forget family and friends, their often excellent record in college, in scouting and other organizations, their plans for the future, and suddenly kill other human beings like themselves?" We don't always ask the question in that manner. Sometimes we are likely to think, almost smugly: "How different those horrible creatures are from the rest of us. How fortunate I am that I could never kill or hurt other people like they did."

I do not like to stop and, in the silence, look within, but when I do I hear a pounding on the floor of my soul. When I open the trap door into the deep darkness I see the monsters emerge for me to deal with. There emerges the sheer mindless destructive brutality of the Frankenstein monster, and next the deft and skilled Aztec priest sacrificing his victim. Then I see the image of the slave trader with his whips and chains and then Torquemada fresh from having burned his witch and then the accuser crying at me with a condemning voice. How painful it is to bear all this, but it is there to bear in all of us. Freud called it the death wish, Jung the demonic darkness. If I do not deal with it, it deals with me. The cross reminds me of all this.

This inhumanity of human to human is tamed most of the time by law and order in most of our communities, but there are not laws strong enough to make men and women simply cease their cruelty and bitterness. There are laws against striking one another, against physical torture, but human beings still pour out their hatred in more acceptable ways. How much of this is done by careless gossip. The cruelty and jealousy, the venom and bitterness, violence and revenge which people sow with their tongues. . . . the misery and pain and suffering that are caused by talking and little acts of hate . . . it is incalculable. The cross reminds us what the human being does to others when one's nature is seized by the demons which dwell below, demons of hate, resentment, bitterness, lust, vindictiveness . . . it symbolizes what ordinary people do when they fail to see these monsters dwelling deep within their lives. The person who talks viciously or plays the power game is stepping into the path of those who invented and practiced crucifixion. It is not a pretty way.

Some religions turn their backs on human evil or claim that it does not exist except in the human mind and that it should simply be ignored. Christianity says that it can't be ignored, can't be avoided. Evil is not just the absence of good; it is a reality. Jesus came and deliberately walked up to evil, challenged it, and said to it: "Let's see which of us is stronger, you or me." Jesus faced evil and conquered it. Because of this we have a chance in dealing with it.

It is a great problem why there is evil in the world, why brutality and meanness are found in all of us, why people suffer so much pain, sorrow and tragedy. While the Christian can't give an answer to the question "Why?", yet the Christian need not fear the question. If he or she cannot give a rational answer, still he or she can conquer the evil, he or she can transform it.

The cross is really the symbol of humanity's evil at its worst and Jesus transformed that symbol into a symbol of victory and love. Christ took all the worst that humans could do and defeated it. He cared enough to do it. He wagered and he won. He transformed the cross, a symbol of humans' brutal hate, in an amazing transformation, to a symbol of hope and victory, of courage and of love.

This destructiveness within us can seldom be transformed until we squarely face it. This confrontation often leads us into the pit. The empty cross is planted there to remind us that suffering is real but not the end, that victory still is possible and real if we strive on.

The Cross as Subtle Evil

It would be difficult if not impossible for any of us to assist in an execution so brutal as a crucifixion. The very thought of doing such things to a human being sends shivers of horror through us. "Whatever else I might do," you say to yourself, "this I would never do. I would never be capable of crucifying a man" . . . And yet are we so sure? We delegate the pulling of the switch, the dropping of the gas pellet to another person. We could never do anything like that. But are we so humane? We deputize someone to take our place. Do we have any right to ask another to do what we won't do? Could you pull that switch or drop the pellet? No, but someone does it for us to relieve us from the guilt. . . . We are so civilized, on the surface.

I shall never forget what happened in a junior college Spanish class in Southern California the day they put Caryl Chessman to death. The last gasp program was on the radio. The class stopped; the program blared out how he looked and how he gasped and slumped. And only one in the class (including the teacher) objected. This was in an American junior college. . . . gloating over a man's death, enjoying, feeling righteous ... letting him bear their darkness and their sin. Shades of the scapegoat ... We are so civilized. Our Father help us bear ourselves.

Let's look at the people who brought Jesus of Nazareth to crucifixion. They were not monsters, but ordinary men and women like you and me ... with little faults, faults which cumulatively led to this man dying on the cross. Who was responsible for this crucifixion? The Roman soldiers? Pilate? the Sanhedrin? Caiaphas? the false witnesses? Judas? the indifferent mob? the nameless carpenter who made the cross? Each and every one of them was responsible. Every one of these individuals had to cooperate to make possible the scene on Golgotha.

Pilate receives most of the blame for Jesus' death, and yet Pilate didn't want to crucify the man. It is true that he pronounced sentence, but he first tried every legal method to release the man. Pilate could see that the man hadn't done anything worthy of death. Pilate may have been cruel and vicious and insensitive, but Pilate wasn't stupid. He saw clearly that the Sanhedrin wanted Jesus out of the way because he was a religious nuisance, an embarrassment to the officials of the Temple.

Why did Pilate condemn Jesus? Because Pilate was a coward. He was afraid of what Caiaphas and the priestly party might do to him if they took this story with their own interpretation to Caesar. He had already tangled with the Jewish hierarchy and he knew their power. They had already gone to Caesar once and Pilate had been warned not to antagonize them again. It was easier to condemn this man than to suffer possible disgrace himself. And after all, what was one harebrained Jewish prophet more or less. . . . Pilate condemned Jesus because he cared more about his comfortable position than he did about justice. He didn't have the courage to stand for what he knew was right. It was because of this relatively small flaw in Pilate's character that Jesus died on a cross. . . . Whenever you and I are willing to sacrifice someone else for our own benefit, whenever we don't have the courage to stand up for what we see is right, we step into the same course that Pilate took, the course which led to Jesus' death. . . . What would you or I have done in Pilate's position? Are we so much better?

And Caiaphas, was he such a monster? Far from it. He was the admired and revered religious leader of the most religious people in that ancient world. He was the High Priest. His personal habits were impeccable. He was a devout and sincerely religious gentleman. He was an excellent administrator, a model family man. Why did he seek to have Jesus condemned? He did it for the simple reason that he was too rigid. He didn't believe that God could be revealed in any other way than through the Holy Scriptures and the Temple services. This man, Jesus, upset what was most holy and valuable to him. He broke the sabbath and cleansed the Temple. He spoke with the authority of God himself, and worst of all, thousands were taking him seriously.

Caiaphas thought he had to protect God from this man, thought he had to protect the Jewish faith and so he said: "It is good for one man to die instead of a nation being destroyed." He was afraid, too, that the followers of this prophet might cause trouble and the Temple would lose the privileges which Rome had granted. Caiaphas' essential flaw was that he thought he had the whole truth; Jesus questioned part of this truth, and therefore he had to be destroyed. People who have fought religious wars, those who have persecuted in the name of religion have followed in his footsteps. Those who put their creeds above mercy and kindness and love, walk there even now.... This quality of character which crucified Jesus is still much abroad in our world. It is easier to be God than to have one.

The members of the Sanhedrin sat and watched the farce of a trial which was called in the middle of the night. A few of them had been taken into Caiaphas' confidence, but the great majority who passed sentence upon this man simply didn't think. They were carried away by the enthusiasm of the accusers and never really considered the matter critically until the next day. And the few who did think and saw through it, said to themselves: Everyone else is carried away by the accusations. Why should I get up and make a fool of myself? My voice or vote against this sentence won't count.... So they sat still and let the sentence stand.

Every time that you or I are carried away by the enthusiasm of accusers and don't think, we are guilty of this fault of character which led to Jesus' crucifixion. Every time we refuse to speak our piece when we disagree, or fail to register our vote, we share in the very failing which enabled a few individuals to ensure the crucifixion of Jesus of Nazareth.... And how often do we neglect to take our part? In a democracy such as ours the nations's sin is ours.

If Caiaphas hadn't had the cooperation of Judas, he would never have been able to find Jesus and take him by night. And he never would have dared arrest him during the day in the Temple. Too many thought well of Jesus and the risk of rioting would have been too great. Why did Judas betray his master? Judas was impatient. He had been with Jesus for a couple of years. He was sick and tired of waiting around. Judas believed that it was time that Jesus called upon heavenly powers and took control of the situation and threw the Romans out of Palestine. Judas was interested in an earthly kingdom and its establishment. He couldn't wait for it to come. He thought to himself: "If I see that he is turned over to Caiaphas and then to the Romans, I will force his hand and make him call upon God and then we will get this kingdom which he has been talking about." Judas thought he was going to precipitate action.

He wasn't interested in the thirty pieces of silver, at least not primarily. Of course, the motives of all of us are mixed. His fault was that he couldn't wait, that he was impatient, and also that he used bad means to bring about a good end. He was so mortified when he found how wrong he had been that he hanged himself. When we can't wait and we want to push things through, when we think we can accomplish a good end by evil means, we do just what Judas did. When we are in a hurry, we step onto the path of action which in Judas led to the condemnation of Jesus of Nazareth, and yet how often we do just these things. How hard it is to wait and to use only admirable means. Hurry is not only of the devil; it *is* the devil.

The most despicable characters in Jesus' trial were the false witnesses who agreed to testify

83

against this man at the midnight trial. They told falsehoods in order to gain something for themselves. They garbled what Jesus had said and swore that he said it just as they related it. Perhaps they were sincere (although it is hard to believe that they were) and had just got the story all mixed up. . . . Sincere or not, these words of gossip turned the tide in the Sanhedrin and brought the condemnation. Their false witness was only gossip in a court, but still gossip, official gossip. . . . Whenever we use words as they did, words of accusation or condemnation, and are not absolutely sure about their truth, then we act as these people who crucified the prophet of Galilee. And how many of the unkind words we speak and hear abroad in the streets of Los Angeles or Chicago, or Atlanta or South Bend are *precisely true?*

Then there was the nameless carpenter who made the cross. He was a skilled workman. He knew full well what the purpose of that cross was. If you questioned him he probably would have said: "But I am a poor man who must make a living. If other men use it ill, is it my fault?" So say all of us who pursue jobs which add nothing to human welfare or which hurt some people. Does the work I do aid or hinder human beings? Are we crossmakers for our modern world? There are many, many of them.

The Roman soldiers were only carrying out their orders, doing their duty. It was not for them to ask who they crucified or why. And, yet, had they not nailed this man to the cross he would not have been nailed there. Of course they might have suffered death had they failed to do the bidding of the governor, but which would have been the better action? There are times when conscience must revolt against duty, for duty to our class or our profession or our country may make crucifiers of us all. To whom and to what do we owe our first allegiance? If we fail to answer this, we walk the same path as those soldiers did.

With all this stacked against him, Jesus still wouldn't have been crucified except for the indifferent mob of people in Jerusalem who didn't care what happened to this man. Only a few hundred could have prevailed upon Caiaphas, the Sanhedrin or Pilate, but they didn't care enough to rouse themselves. He was a fine man. They had heard him, they admired him, but they weren't there to shout *Jesus* instead of *Barabbas*. They didn't try to protest. They didn't rouse themselves from bed that morning. Hard to get up in the morning. Warm beds. Indifference to Jesus. Is it nothing to all you that pass by? Indifference to Jesus was what led to his crucifixion as much as anything else and those who today are indifferent follow in the footsteps of those who made possible the greatest injustice of all time. There is no force which harms or hinders the work of Jesus more today *than pure indifference*, not caring enough to be for him or against. . . . It is sometimes the very attitude we can have, the most destructive force there is.

These were the things that crucified Jesus on Friday in passover week A.D. 29. They were not wild viciousness or sadistic brutality or naked hate, but the civilized vices of cowardice, bigotry, impatience, timidity, falsehood, indifference . . . vices all of us share . . . the very vices which crucify human beings today. Perhaps we too might have helped to crucify him had we been there. The cross shows us the qualities in each of us which

85

make for destruction, crucifixion. These are the masks that the monsters of the deep assume to deceive civilized men and women.

The cross helps us measure our lives correctly, our little daily trespasses and faults. How much they cost both humans and God. They lead to war and riot. They break men and women, driving them to mental illness and to crime. They also nailed Jesus of Nazareth to a cross.

The Cross as Christ's Humanity

Jesus of Nazareth suffered upon the cross and died there like any person who suffers and dies. The nails tore his hands, the awful agony pierced his body and soul. He was a person just like you and me. He shares our lot; he knew our condition. He was one with us. The cross demonstrates his humanity as nothing else could demonstrate it.

Had Jesus just disappeared one fine spring day by ascending into heaven without having known the cross, one might wonder if indeed he were a man at all. He had tremendous power ... he healed the sick, he raised the dead, he walked upon water, he spoke with an authority which came from great depths. His wisdom never has been fathomed. There was something unearthly about him, something which struck into the hearts of men and women and made them stop in wonder and amazement. The cross stands there to remind us that he was still a person just like you and me. He knew what it was to have the fatigue and hindrances of these clumsy and often unreliable bodies. He was not a God masquerading as a person, but a person who knew all that we suffer through, all our temptations and weaknesses.

So often we forget that Jesus lived a normal human life as we do, that he played with the village boys in Nazareth, that he held the home together for his brothers and sisters until his brothers were able to take over, that he went to the village weddings and parties. We forget that he was tempted after his baptism, just as we are tempted . . . and he went for forty days in the wilderness.

The Christian religion would lose its power to console us if Jesus were not a real man in every sense of the word. If Jesus were not a full, real human being, then God would never really understand the lot we bear, our darkness and our pain, our suffering, anxiety and ignorance, our weakness and our temptations. Then we would be separated from him by a great gulf and we could not be sure that he cares or understands. It is the cross which tells us, in a way so dramatic that no man or woman who will look can fail to see it, that God in Christ does understand and does care. We have a God who cared enough to be one with us. His words don't come to us out of a cold and unsympathetic heart, but from one who knew the worst of human pain.

As Shakespeare suggested, it is not difficult to bear other people's toothaches; but when one's own jaw is throbbing, that is another matter. We will listen to Jesus Christ, for he spoke from the darkness at the Cross. We may not understand him or agree with him or obey him, but nobody can challenge his right to speak. He was a person and so no person is a stranger to him. He was a person in the deepest and most painful sense of being one.

We have a God who cared enough about us to become a person and accept what that meant. Is there any greater love than this? And suffering with us I am sure he came to love us more, if more were possible, for it is out of suffering commonly borne and carried that the greatest love springs forth. If he had been only some great figure high in the heavens it would be hard to return him much love, much devotion, but to one who has suffered more than we for no evil that he did, to such a one our love can pour out unstintedly, richly, naturally and we can be consoled. We feel as though we are not alone and we suffer not in vain. . . .

How important to us that he was a man and suffered as we do . . . and there are four unmistakable evidences that he suffered. His soul was wracked when he prayed in the Garden of Gethsemane. When he could still have turned away and fled, he chose to stay and wait for Judas and the Temple guard. Great drops of sweat appeared upon his brow and fell like blood, so great and terrible was his agony. There he faced straight on the full impact of human evil, accepted the full human condition and entered the final struggle . . . and waited.

Also he suffered through the night of buffeting and buffoonery, through the trial and mocking by the soldiers, through his scourging . . . How do we know? Because he was so weak from the pain and agony . . . for physical and mental pain can sap our strength just as disease does . . . that he could not carry the cross beam up the Via Dolorosa, but he stumbled and fell three times, and finally another had to carry the cross for him. And even then he could hardly make his way up the hill.

And when he arrived there he turned aside the cup of herbs which would have numbed him partially to the pain, because he knew his task was to drain this cup of humanity to its dregs, so that no one could say they suffered more than he . . . so that there might be no sufferer who could not look upon him as a brother.

Hanging there he cried out: "I thirst." Why this cry? We have listened to one of the stories of those who knew traumatic thirst, the thirst which comes to the fragile human being because of the loss of body fluids. How many times among the dying on a battlefield have been heard from the wounded the words "Some water . . . I thirst . . . A drink . . ." How often the last words of the dying are the same. I have often heard them. In these words are carried the fullness of physical pain and suffering. They are the epitome of this agony, its essence.

Physical pain is not, however, the worst that we can bear, but rather mental and spiritual pain, and in literature there is no darker or more despairing cry than his: "Eloi, Eloi, lama sabachthani . . . My God, my God, why hast thou forsaken me?" The light had gone out in his soul and there was nothing then but the heavy and crushing darkness. . . . in physical torture, forsaken by his friends and followers, ridiculed by the religious leaders of his people, mocked by the crowd, and then deserted by the very God who led him there. Is it any wonder some believe that his heart broke from the pain of it? They maintain that this was the direct cause of his death, an inner dissolution, a broken heart and life.

Every one of us has times when we pass through inner darkness, when the light seems to go out of our souls and we are blind and broken and life seems to be a broken vessel. We seem to be tormented by shadowy monsters and there is no light at all. We are terrified and hopeless. This is worse than physical pain, for there is a limit to physical pain. In shock we black out and become unconscious. There is a limit beyond which we can feel no more, but this inner blackness and meaninglessness, to this there seems to be no limit, no bottom. Indeed most suicide is an attempt to escape the inner pain and darkness of the soul and to take death instead, so oppressive and destructive can this pain be. Physical pain alone seldom drives human beings to this action.

And Jesus plumbed this to the depth, to the very depth. He knew human agony at its deepest and worst. And while most of us in our suffering can look back and see how we have helped create it, how we deserve some of our suffering, in this one there was no reason that he should suffer. His only goal had been to bring men and women life, and this is what they did to him. No wonder the blackness closed in around him. I doubt that any other has suffered more than Jesus did on Golgotha.

There is a power released whenever human beings are willing to suffer undeservedly for others. I believe he offered this suffering up to God as a sacrifice for those who betrayed, ignored, and crucified him. When a man or woman does this, suffering loses its totally destructive aspect and becomes rather one of the most creative forces in the world. There are few powers on earth greater than the power of unmerited suffering gladly borne for another.

Throughout the ages the great Christians have followed in Jesus' footsteps and suffered gladly for others, and the effect of such suffering is never lost. This is what Stephen did when they stoned him. Paul standing by was not unaffected. This is what the early Christians did when their masters persecuted them and killed them. They offered this suffering to God on behalf of their persecutors, and their masters were often transformed.

There is an incredible power in suffering used like this. It is the power of vicarious suffering, of substitutionary love.

James Nayler showed the same spirit. On his way home from prison for his religious conviction he was set upon by thieves and brutally wounded. A few hours before he died he said these words: "There is a spirit which I feel that delights to do no evil, nor to revenge any wrong, but delights to endure all things, in hope to enjoy its own in the end. Its hope is to outlive all wrath and contention, and to weary out all exaltation and cruelty, or whatever is of a nature contrary to itself. . . . I found it alone, being forsaken. I have fellowship therein with them who lived in dens and desolate places in the earth, who through death obtained this resurrection and eternal holy life." James Nayler had caught the spirit of Jesus on the cross.

The naked suffering and agony of the cross speak a message of great significance. They tell us that we are not alone in our physical and mental pain and darkness. God in Christ is there with us too. He knows and cares.

The cross helps us to love him as we gaze upon the suffering he bore, for it is easy for our hearts to go out in love to one who has suffered so. I wonder if we could really love Jesus as we sometimes do if he hadn't suffered on the cross. Real love so often springs from suffering borne together.

The cross gives us the secret which enables us to suffer creatively when suffering strikes. . . .

The cross tells us again and again that God cared enough for us to suffer all this in Christ for us. He was willing to humble himself and become a man. The cross is a symbol of Christ's humanity. What love it is which takes this agony upon itself willingly for us. . . . what love. No wonder Unamuno wrote that the chief sanctity of a temple is that it is a place where men and women can gather to weep together.

The Cross as Love

The man who hung from the center cross was different from most crucified men. He didn't scream and curse and bellow like a wounded bull. Most victims did. For the first three hours he hung there silently, patiently, a quiet dignity about him. There was no doubt about the pain he suffered; his face portrayed that. But he didn't give way to it or allow the agony to undo him. If he had, we probably wouldn't be meditating upon what he did.

For three hours, silence . . . . the silence that judges by saying nothing; and then seven utterances, amazing utterances. If ever anyone had cause to be bitter and curse humankind, it was Jesus as he hung there. His essential will and desire had been to bring human beings a deeper knowledge of God, to enable them to find the key to real living by loving one another and opening themselves to God's spirit, and this is what they did. They crucified him. And how did he respond? With nothing but love . . . each of these words reflected love. He cared for them even though they crucified him as they did. He made the cross a symbol of love by pouring forth a healing spring of divine concern when most people would have cried out in bitterness and anger or simply screamed in agony or cursed.

"Father, forgive them, for they know not what they do." These were the incredible first words which issued from his lips. A prayer for those who were destroying him. "Do not hold this against them, Father," he said in effect, "for they don't understand." For whom did he pray this prayer that day? For all of those who conspired to bring him to this end. . . . for Caiaphas, for Judas, for Pilate, for the Roman soldiers, for the indifferent crowd that let him down, for the sadistic mob which hooted and howled around him now, for his faithless disciples who fled like clucking chickens. Father, forgive them all.

I keep a crucifix in my office. When I feel that the world has been hard on me or that my job is impossible or people have been unfair, I look at the crucifix and I say to myself: "You feel sorry for yourself, you who deserve so much of this which has come upon you. There is one who did no wrong and look at what they did to him, and think of his response. . . . What's so bad about your lot?" It is hard to feel sorry for myself when I keep a crucifix there before my eyes and think of what the cross means. It is hard to strike out in revenge or bitterness if first my glance falls upon the figure on the cross and I pause to think for a moment. If he could love under such circumstances, then perhaps I can love in these. It is good to have a crucifix hanging somewhere in sight.

The power of Jesus is amazing; the contagion of his life is incredible. One thinks of Stephen and the whole army of martyrs who followed him, men and women able to forgive their persecutors. The early Christian church followed the way of Jesus and they conquered. It is difficult for an enemy to strike out brutally again after being forgiven by the object of that brutality. There was indeed a power in those words of Jesus, a tremendous power, a power we can have.

His first word was to his persecutors; the second to a lost and broken man seeking help. Both of the other criminals cursed and screamed during their crucifixion. They laughed at the man between them whom the high priests came to mock, but gradually one of them grew silent. He began to think, for pain can make the mind quite clear. "Perhaps he is the one. . . . perhaps he is the person whom some say he is. . . ." The quiet dignity, the patience, and then this first word of love and power made its impact, and so the criminal cried out: "Jesus, remember me when you come in your kingly power." There was no hesitation in his response, no waiting to consider; instead the words came directly forth: "Truly, I say to you, today you will be with me in Paradise." It is never too early or too late. Jesus' love flows out to anyone who wishes it, who seeks it. If ever a person waited until late to ask, it was this man about to die, pinioned to a cross, having just cursed the one he now sought out. But Jesus did not hesitate.

Here on the cross we find a love to the lost and broken. Love is difficult for us to give, you and me, under ordinary circumstances when we have time to think, but here on the cross it flowed naturally from him, amazing love. Jesus' love doesn't wait until we have earned it; it flows out to all who will receive it, or ask for it. Here is prayer and its answer. Is not prayer turning to

Christ in need, as someone has suggested, no matter what the circumstances? No question about worth or value, just need, and then love is given. How often he puts us to shame. How seldom the church follows his example on the cross. How do we view the dregs of human beings? Do we welcome them, reach out to bring them in? Sometimes the worst human beings are most easily touched here at the cross.

Then looking down he saw his mother and his friend. It was probably harder for him to look on them than any of the others. How his heart must have been torn to see them there, but there was no bitterness, no remorse, just more love for those who had cared for him and for whom he cared so deeply. He said: "Woman, behold your son!" and then looking at the young man standing there, "Behold your mother!" What he said was really something like this: "I have cared for you both. These close relationships have meant much to me, my family and my friends. Carry them on for me. As I have cared for you, continue on, that my love may not be lost. I care for you more than you know: so care for one another." Words of love to his mother and his closest friend, words of consolation, words which would help them through the dark days ahead. No words ever sanctified the human family or human friendship more than these.

There was a time of silence as the black clouds tumbled and darkened the sky in outraged sympathy for this man's blackness. It was out of this darkness that the next two cries broke forth: "My God, my God, why hast thou forsaken me?" and then, "I thirst." Words of love, too, in a real sense, words which showed that he loved us enough to suffer on the cross for you and me. Better than any others these words demonstrate the care, the love, which prompted the son of God to become a man. He cared enough for men and women that he was willing to suffer even this, even this.

The afternoon was wearing on when he spoke again. A stillness reigned; nature waited breathlessly. The end was near. Twice he spoke and then his head fell forward; the brutality was done. "Father, into thy hands I commend my spirit," came clearly, though quietly from his lips. The blackness had passed, the light was beginning to break, and in words of trust he turned to the Father who but a little while before had disappeared and who he thought had forsaken him. These words spoke trusting love, the love of the hurt child who runs to mother or father, knowing that there is safety in their arms. And then the words: "It is finished." His job was completed. He had loved in light and darkness, in pain and trouble and joy, and having loved to the end he gave up the spirit with a sigh and died. God's love for human beings had run its course, had done its utmost, and now the task was done.

Why is the cross important? Because it shows God's love for people as nothing else in heaven or earth. God cared enough to endure even this to manifest his love for men and women, and on the cross, in the worst that humans could do, still this love poured out. Not even the worst that people could do could dam up its flow or make it cease.

When I would like to be assured of God's love, I look at the cross. Had it been endured merely with patient forbearance, it would have demonstrated love. But how much more than this happened on the cross. Here are words of love for all people, the lost, the loved ones, the persecutors.

He lived as he had taught others to live. Most people would have simply pitied themselves. He preached love, he taught it, he lived it, he died it. The cross is the demonstration of Christ's love for people, its richest symbol. We would never dare dream of the depth of God's love for us had there been no cross. The cross gave Christ an opportunity to manifest the depth of his love, its unfathomable richness. On the cross Christ showed what God is really like, how loving, how compassionate. The cross means love. This is why that day is called Good Friday.

The Cross as Courage

Love without strength can be weak and ineffectual. The love of Jesus attained its incredible power and effectiveness because it was compounded with another quality as near to the heart and nature of God as love itself. Strange how we can look at the cross, at all it was, at what Jesus did upon it, and often fail to see the courage of the man. It was his courage as well as his love which led him there and left him hanging on the cross. It was his courage which enabled him to love in those last dark hours. The victory which was won there on Golgotha was compounded of three precious elements, of humility (he was willing to become a man and suffer), of love through which he expressed the very nature of God, and of courage.

The courage of that man! He walked willingly into death in its most excruciating form. He accepted without flinching the condemnation of his people's religious leaders. He entered into the abyss of the darkness of our human meaninglessness and cried out: "My God, my God, why hast thou forsaken me?"

Jesus was no village fool caught unawares by these tragic forces of evil and destroyed by them against his will. Jesus knew full well what the path was that he took. He knew the animosity of the Temple authorities, knew what his chances were after he deliberately cleansed the Temple. He walked deliberately, and of his own free choice, into the crucifixion at the place of the skull.

He had the courage to live out the deepest level of his life. He affirmed his own essential being. He knew what was the right and the true way for him. Few deny that he had wisdom to know what was right, but more than that, he had the courage to stand by it, no matter what forces in heaven or in hell opposed him. He lived as he knew he ought. He was true to the essence of his own being in spite of the ridicule of the crowd, in spite of the opposition of the authorities, in spite of the cross which stood before him, in spite of death and fear, in spite of castigation by the leaders of his people, in spite of the agony and blackness of his own soul. This is the real meaning of courage.

This takes more grit and fortitude, more power of will, than simply enduring physical pain or stepping into danger. Real courage is a quiet and determined thing. It is neither loud nor boasting. It is not foolhardy. Real courage is the firm unyielding resolution to live out the intimations of eternity we have within us no matter what forces of destruction throw themselves against us, no matter into what darkness they take us, no matter what may happen.

This is real courage and this quality of life is dear to God. It is difficult to find God unless one stays close to the deepest element of one's life and follows it through no matter what comes. Courage doesn't mean an absence of fear, but a willingness to go on in spite of fear. Real light is only found on the other side of darkness of despair and bereavement, of pain and turmoil, of anxiety and guilt, and to pass through darkness we need courage. Courage enables us to break out of the shell in which we are confined as a chrysalis and to become what we truly are and soar high into life which can be. We can love and be humble all our lives, but until we add courage to these other qualities, our lives are bound to fail.

In Jesus we see one of the most dramatic and magnificent examples of courage that has ever been shown to the human race.

Jesus need not have been hanging on the cross had he not willed it. He could easily have avoided it. We need to remember this. It is this which makes the cross magnificent; it was a free offering of a person for all human beings. He started on a way which led to the cross and at any time he could have left it.

If he hadn't come to Bethany, right under the nose of the high priests, and raised Lazarus from the dead, he wouldn't have forced the Temple hierarchy to take notice of him. But a voice within him said: "Mary and Martha grieve and it is more important to be true to the love within you, more important to show people what God can do, than to worry about what humans can do." He listened to the voice and he went to Bethany and he raised Lazarus, and his fate was sealed.

If he hadn't turned his face toward Jerusalem at this time, but simply stayed away from the holy city for a while, the storm might have passed and he might have avoided what he finally met. But there was a whisper within which said: "Go forth and witness. Do not hide your light. Should God fear man? The place for the prophet is in the holy city. The nation assembles there to eat the passover." Jesus heard that whisper and, though he knew what lay in store for him in Jerusalem, he had the courage to go up.

If Jesus hadn't entered Jerusalem as he did on Palm Sunday, but had quietly crept in by the side gate, the High Priest might not have noticed him. But he came triumphantly, proclaiming his entrance, proclaiming his prophetic role, and no one in Jerusalem could ignore him.

If Jesus had simply stood by and ignored the corruption in the Temple, the graft and crookedness of the money-changers and those who sold animals for sacrifice, he might even then have escaped. But a voice within him said: "You cannot compromise with this. This is the house of God and they are making it a den of thieves." Jesus heard this voice and he spoke these words and he drove out the animals and the money-changers, and in so doing he threw down the gauntlet. This the authorities could not ignore. It was a deliberate affront and insult to those who ran the Temple and to the religious lives of Israel. What courage this man had!

Jesus could have fled in the dark Judean night from the garden of Gethsemane as his human nature cried out for him to do. But he prayed and he listened, and the voice within him said: "The way of courage and of love and of humility is to stand by and let them try to destroy you. This is my will that men and women may learn by you the way of life. Those who seek to gain their lives shall lose them and those who lose their lives shall gain them." I am so grateful that he had the courage to wait there and reply: "Not my will but thine be done."

If Christ had tried to defend himself before Pilate and the Sanhedrin, he would have stooped to the methods which were used against him. How different were Jesus and Paul as they each faced trial. How much more the man was Jesus. A voice spoke within Jesus as he stood before these men which said: "You are really the judge, not they. Ignore them. Be still. In this silence the nobility of your life will show forth more than by words." He heeded that voice, and with a dignity which people have worshipped for nearly two thousand years, he stood silently before his accusers and let them strike him down.

If Jesus had taken the cup of gall and let himself be numbed upon the cross, he too would probably have screamed out as the other two, but he had the courage to face human cruelty as it was. Even though his body cried out within him, he had the courage to be still upon the cross and then to speak out in words of love. This was the final test of his courage, his greatest feat.

His way was the way of love and truth with no compromise at all. He had the courage to affirm this, the deepest and best within him, in spite of the threats of death and condemnation and dark meaninglessness. He walked into the darkness until the light faded, and it was pitch dark, and still he walked on resolutely. He came to the end of his rope and he hung on; still he hung on. Here was real courage. Here was an example of what a real person really is.

Why did God raise him up?

It was because he was willing to suffer humbly for others. He was willing to pour a stream of love under all conditions. He had courage.

So often I need to remember that courage is near the heart of God, and the really courageous are dear to him whether they seek him or not. Like those who love, they share in the very nature of God.

Those who would conquer, let them have in them the mind which was in Christ Jesus. He was willing to let himself be humbled unto that death on a cross because he loved. He had the courage to struggle through the darkness. Those who follow this example with the help of his Spirit, they will find God waiting to receive them into the eternal arms and they will hear him say: "Well done, good and faithful servant. You have finished your appointed task."

The Cross as Hope

Jesus spoke twice more, this time words of hope and confidence, of victory and joy: "Father, into your hands I commend my spirit" and, "It is finished." Then Jesus gave a sigh and his head fell forward, his chin upon his chest. The soldiers who kept watch there thought that he was unconscious, but his mother and his friend who stood by in agony, watching—they knew that death had come. There is no mistaking death if you care about the dying. Something breaks and flees and we are left with lifeless husks.

Mary and John and the women who stood there dissolved in tears. They had tried so hard to be ready for this. For six hours they knew that separation would come and he would die. At first they had hoped for legions of angels or some other miracle, but as the day wore on and he suffered and died like any other, their hope gave way. He was an ordinary man and he died an ordinary death, more loving and heroic than most, yet he died as an ordinary mortal dies. It was all over. Even though they had expected death, even longed for it for his sake, when it came it was a shock.

Death is always sudden. People are seldom prepared for it. There is something mysterious about it, something strange and final which undoes us and makes us tremble and then we give way to tears. So it was with those friends of Jesus. They cried until they could cry no more and then they waited. How unfortunate are those who cannot weep.

The rest of what they saw came to them through a haze more like a dream than life. Their light had gone out; their hope had died; their joy was extinguished. They were dead with him and yet alive. Those who have suffered great bereavement know what I describe. The light had gone out in them.

They saw the messenger come from Pilate with orders that the legs of the victims were to be smashed so that they might die and be taken down. The religious authorities had made arrangements for this action so that the bodies would not defile the Sabbath. They were careful about their religious duties. The soldiers did their duty. They tried to appear indifferent, but the vigil of suffering had undone them too and they were glad when it was over. The hammer-like blows added little to the pain of the suffering ones and within a few minutes the two on the outside crosses were dead.

The soldiers were surprised when they found that Jesus was already dead. One of them threw a spear at the body to make sure. There was no reaction. He was dead. Water and blood poured from the pierced side. The centurion sent his report. The three men were dead and those who wished to claim the bodies could come and get them.

John and the women stood there helplessly.

They could not take down the body, and they had no place to put it when it was removed. They couldn't take it home. Remember the horror the Jews had of the bodies of the dead; of all unclean things dead bodies were the worst. In muted whispers they talked over what they might do, and then the matter was taken from their hands. A man of wealth and prominence brought his servants and took the body down. It was Joseph of Arimathaea. John and the women knew him. He had come secretly often to talk with Jesus.

They watched him tenderly take the body. It was no easy task to remove the lifeless form of a man weighing some 180 pounds. The servants finally pulled the hands and feet free from the nails and laid him on the ground. They had brought a winding sheet and silently they wrapped the lifeless form within the shroud. They had brought a napkin to place around his head.

The women followed Joseph and his servants to a nearby garden where Joseph had had a new tomb hewn from rock, a simple tomb, one Joseph had planned for his own burial. Joseph was an old man. This was a great gift. Tombs were as expensive then as they are now. Inside the tomb they laid him on a stone slab and then it took four servants to roll the huge stone to close the opening of the tomb.

The story was finished. The tale was done. He whom they loved was dead and buried and so the handful of mourners dispersed. Each went his own way. The women went to get spices to embalm him, to perform one last labor of love. John went to find the disciples. The seven whom we met earlier went out to share the things that they had found.

John found the disciples dejectedly huddled together in a cheerless room. One candle gave them all their light. He had trouble getting in. The doors were barred, the shutters closed and locked. Here was a broken and defeated band of people afraid the Temple guard might be there at the door for them, ashamed of their fear, their hopes broken, guilty for their faithlessness the night before. They had hoped up until the last for a miracle. They had felt the earthquake and seen the storm. And they had wondered. But John was there to describe for them the things which had actually happened. The master, their hope and their life, was dead and buried. The life they had admired for the last three years had been a joke, a tragic illusion. They had been deceived, duped. It was all a dream and the dawn had come, revealing only a barren wasteland. Their hearts were broken; their hopes were extinguished; they were drowned in futility and meaninglessness; they were lost in darkness.

Is this the end of our story? If it were, Good Friday would be the most tragic day of all days and there would be no church or Christian faith. We would not now be praising here in silent fantasy. Good Friday is meaningless without what happened two days later, just as the Christian faith is meaningless without what happened on Sunday, the first day of the week.

For another lonely, hopeless, gloomy day these men dwelt mutely together. They hardly spoke. They were big, strong, hearty peasants, most of them, and they too wept until they could weep no more. Men were allowed to be more human then. Singly they began making their plans. This one back to his fishing, another to his accounts, another to his farm. No one would ever deceive them again.

Then the miracle occurred. It was Sunday morning. There was an excited knock on the door and there stood one of the women. Breathlessly she told them that they had gone to the tomb early in the morning before it was even light and they had found the stone gone from before the tomb. It was the last indignity. They couldn't even leave his bones in peace. John and Peter ran with the women, ran as fast as they could go. They reached the tomb. The stone was gone. The winding cloth and the napkin which had been around his head lay there folded. It did not have the look of grave robbers.

A glimmer of hope began to rise in John's heart, not yet in his mind, but in his heart. Could it be? Could it be? Before he could answer this question the reports began to flood in upon them. Mary Magdalene came with radiant face, weeping for joy: "He is risen. I have seen him. He is not dead!" Wandering from the garden of the tomb these two came upon Mary the mother of James and Salome. The women were ecstatic: "We went to the tomb and found two young men of dazzling appearance who said that we should not seek him there, but that he had risen from the dead." These two disciples questioned them. Why were they so sure? "If you had seen them," they said, "you would understand. He is more alive than he ever was before. He is life itself."

The disciples were struck dumb when Peter and John returned. They knew not what they believed, and then, as they wondered, as they vacillated between fear and hope, as they talked and questioned, Cleopas came running to the hiding place. They let him in and barred the door again. "I have seen him, I have seen him," he cried. "He walked with us and our hearts burned, and then he turned aside to have supper with us, and as he broke the bread suddenly our eyes were opened and we saw him. It was Jesus, only glorified and a million times more wonderful than before; and then he disappeared. . . ."

As Cleopas spoke a chill of fear gripped the room. One by one they looked toward the door. They supposed they saw a spirit and then the master spoke: "Why are you troubled, and why do questionings arise in your hearts? See my hands and my feet, that it is I myself. Handle me and see; for a spirit has not flesh and bones as you see that I have."

Jesus suffered. Jesus conquered. God raised him up. If such a man can rise again is there not hope for you and me and for those whom we have loved and lost? Need we fear anything if he has suffered all these things and conquered them for us? Is there not hope for us?

Neither death nor condemnation, neither futility nor pain need hold us in bondage any longer. He has conquered and we can conquer with him.

The Cross as Decision

Here is the message of the cross. The best man faced the worst death with patience in the presence of every provocation, with love which never gave way to bitterness, with courage which carried him through the very depth of blackness and despair.

This event on the Friday before the passover Sabbath A.D. 29 in Jerusalem was either the most irredeemable tragedy that ever occurred or it was the greatest victory ever won for human beings. Either it convinces us that we lead a futile struggle against a hostile or indifferent world that always ends in defeat and disaster; or, else, it tells us that God in Christ conquered the worst that hell and earth could pour upon him and that he gives us a way to conquer with Him. The cross has in fact two messages and it depends upon us which we take . . . the message of despair or the message of victory. It is one or the other.

If Christ died upon the cross and that was the end, if there was no resurrection, as many maintain, then the cross points up the ultimate meaninglessness of life, the utter pointlessness of trying to follow love, of living close to God, of ever trying to become whole, complete. Then we can expect no justice in this life or in the hereafter, no love, no mercy, no fulfillment. Then we find ourselves up against a cold, indifferent universe of slowly dying stars, which cares for nothing. Then there is no hand which can ever set things aright, and the passion for justice and love in us is but a dream which never can or will be fulfilled. We die and are extinguished and whether we are good or bad, evil, malicious, hateful, or kindly, generous, patient, loving, courageous makes no difference, none at all. The dead material universe slumbers on and cares not in the least. Mechanical atoms or blind forces or electrical charges care naught for human beings, for their virtue or their wickedness. What we do is all in vain and dies with us and the slowly dying stars gleam coldly on.

This is what life would be like if Christ died upon the cross and that was all. Then those who say: "Let's eat, drink and be merry, for tomorrow we die," have the right answer. Then it is a matter of getting what we can for ourselves, snatching what pleasure and peace and comfort we can from the hands of others and savoring it until the end. If there were no resurrection, this is the consistent and sensible response to the cross and life. It is then the part of good sense to gain as much power and strength as we can, for we can count only on ourselves. We must build fortresses large enough and strong enough to keep others out and pile them high with the things that we want against the day of disaster or trouble or famine. We must trust no one, for anyone may be a Judas. We must live isolated, hemmed in, self-sufficient, detached, apart, caring nothing for others. Otherwise we may become entangled in life and find ourselves conquered, crucified. And remember, if Christ was allowed to die and be extinguished, can we who are so much less good and whole expect anything much better? If God didn't raise up Jesus from the dead, then he won't raise up anyone and then there probably isn't any God at all. There isn't anyone, any power in this universe who cares.

We are then at the mercy of human brutality, at the mercy of our own and other people's inhumanity to human beings. Men and women angry at the universe for making life so difficult for them strike out against their own kind and try to relieve their suffering by making others suffer. Humankind which is the subject of cruelty and hatred and meanness pours the same out upon all who come near them. The Genghis Khans and Attilas are to be expected and admired. Since there isn't enough food to go around, there will always be bloodshed and war and pillage and devastation as people vie with each other to seize with brutality what they cannot otherwise obtain. There will be more and worse wars, atomic explosions, more and worse Dachaus, Buchenwalds and Mai Lais. This is what is before us and there is no way out except to be so strong that you can resist and perish quickly if you can't resist.

This is what life is most probably like if Christ didn't rise from the dead. I am not trying to frighten anybody. I am just trying to be honest and this I must be. Those silly people who talk about the good Jesus and all his fine, uplifting teaching, his high morals and fine example ... those who tell us we ought to be brave and follow his example and walk in his ways, but that we mustn't take seriously the story of his resurrection ... those people are not honest with themselves or others.

Why on earth should we follow Jesus if his way leads only to a cross, if it leads only to suffering and pain, rejection, ridicule, scorn, and then the extinction of death? If Jesus didn't rise again, then there is no folly quite like the folly of following Jesus' footsteps and his way. We are so used to hearing how fine his way is, and how good, and how we ought to follow it, that we seldom stop to think how utterly silly this is if we don't believe that he rose again.

I get quite impatient with these silly people who talk about virtue and goodness and tell us that we should follow these things even if the only life after death is what we pass on to our children. *How really funny such a way of life would be.* If these people would stop and spend a Good Friday on their knees looking at the cross and really feeling it and listening to what it says, then they could never talk like that again. We humans can't look at the cross without seeing the depth and width and power of evil in ourselves. *We can't expect much of ourselves or others without God.*

If Jesus didn't rise again, then Nietzsche was right. The Nazis were right, and the Fascists were right. Dialectic materialism is right. The modern Hitler, black or white or yellow, has the right way. The correct way to live is to find and keep power in one's own hands. That is all the right or wrong there is ... any means to gain an end.

There might be some monumental heroic figures who for the sake of their own suffering might desire to follow Christ, but they are simply deluded, probably mentally ill or nearly so, who somehow enjoy suffering and pain and ridicule. Such individuals should then be pitied. . . . And Jesus the most to be pitied of them all, so sadly deceived, so wrong. He suffered so much for nothing. He counted on help which didn't come, which never comes.

This is the conclusion which flows from the cross and Good Friday if Jesus didn't rise again. This is why so many of us don't want to look at the cross. We are afraid that Jesus didn't rise again and we don't want to see what life is really like if that is so. In the depths of us we know, but we don't want to look at what we know and by keeping busy we can avoid our deeper selves. So often we don't have the guts to face life! How chicken many of us often are. We don't want to make a decision and Good Friday requires a decision. And so we refuse to look at the cross.

Good Friday says to us, when we are still and listen: You can't be complacent. Life isn't a bed of roses. There is malignant evil and suffering in it. If Jesus didn't rise again, then your life is hopeless, your future futile, your dreams shattered. You must make up your mind to live in that kind of world, which takes more strength than any of us have, and accept this blind futility. Either this, or we must take Jesus seriously, take the resurrection seriously. The cross confronts us with alternatives, futile despair or a long and hard way to victory. It blocks off the other ways. Unfortunately no decision is casting our vote for the futile way.

Whenever we really look at life as it is, we see the shadow of the cross lying over us, sometimes as an atomic missile, sometimes as ranging hordes of angry, hungry people, sometimes even as our own foolish, strange co-humans across a breakfast table or a desk. So we don't look. We bury our heads in busyness and hurry and new titillations of material possessions for themselves. Better civilizations than ours have fallen. The almost forgotten Christian empire of Byzantium lasted over a thousand years and disappeared as if it had never been. Will we be next because we will not choose and act?

The cross stands before us . . . It means either a broad and easy way to hopeless futility and destruction or a steep and narrow path to victory for us, and for our nation, our families, and our children.

The cross urges us to decide which way we go if we will look at it. The reason that we don't like to look at the cross is that we don't want to decide. The cross means either doom or hope. It suggests decision.

At the foot of the cross the road forks, one way to darkness, and the other way to light. On the narrow way and steep, there is a light ahead and a hand which reaches out to help any who would come. It's really easier than the other way, for there is more help. The cross tells of one who waits around the bend to bear our burden or even to lift us if we fall, but he does not force any person on this way. The choice is ours . . . it is mine, yours, up to each of us.

BOOKS BY MORTON KELSEY

Tongue Speaking
God, Dreams, and Revelation
Encounter with God
Healing and Christianity
Myth, History and Faith
The Christian and the Supernatural
The Other Side of Silence: A Guide to Christian
    Meditation
Can Christians Be Educated?: A Proposal for Ef-
    fective Communication of Our Christian Reli-
    gion
The Age of Miracles
Dreams: A Way To Listen to God
Tales To Tell: Legends of the Senecas
Afterlife: The Other Side of Dying
Adventure Inward

Booklets
The Art of Christian Love
The Reality of the Spiritual World
Finding Meaning: Guidelines for Counselors